eat the
cookie...
buy the
shoes

eat the cookie...
buy the shoes

GIVING YOURSELF PERMISSION TO LIGHTEN UP

JOYCE MEYER

New York   Boston   Nashville

Unless otherwise indicated, Scriptures are taken from the Amplified® Bible. copyright © 1954, 1962, 1965, 1987 by the Lockman Foundation. Used by permission.

Scriptures noted KJV are taken from the King James Version of the Bible.

Scriptures noted The Message are taken from The Message. Copyright © 1993, 1994, 1995, 1996, 2000, 2001, 2002. Used by permission of NavPress Publishing Group.

Scriptures noted NKJV are taken from the NEW KING JAMES VERSION. Copyright © 1979, 1980, 1982, Thomas Nelson, Inc., Publishers.

FaithWords
Hachette Book Group
237 Park Avenue
New York, NY 10017

www.faithwords.com

Printed in the United States of America

Originally published in hardcover by FaithWords.

First International Trade Edition: April 2010
10 9 8 7 6 5 4 3 2 1

FaithWords is a division of Hachette Book Group, Inc.
The FaithWords name and logo are trademarks of Hachette Book Group, Inc.

ISBN 978-0-446-56995-8

CONTENTS

eat the
cookie...
buy the
shoes

CHAPTER
1

The Cookie

It was Saturday afternoon in St. Louis, Missouri, during our 2007 annual autumn women's convention, and we were on a brief lunch break preceding the final session of the conference. This is one of the most significant events that our ministry sponsors. It is attended by thousands of women from all over the world, and it requires a tremendous amount of hard work, creativity, and preparation. The three-day conference begins on Thursday evening, and by the Saturday lunch break, I'm usually mentally, physically, and emotionally tired. This particular event seems to take a lot out of me for several reasons. By the last session, I feel a great deal of responsibility to be sure that the conference ends in a way that leaves our attendees energized and very glad they came.

We had enjoyed a small lunch, and I was gathering all of my strength getting ready to go to the platform and bring the conference to a fantastic finish. Dave and I were leaving the lunchroom when I saw a plate of chocolate chip cookies I had passed by when I was selecting my lunch from the buffet. As I saw them this time I thought, "I really want (need) a little piece of one of those cookies." I stopped at the table and broke off about one-third of one of the cookies and ate it. As we proceeded to the platform Dave said, "Did you just eat part of that cookie?" His tone of voice was accusing and right away I got defensive. I felt like saying, "Chill out...it is just a piece of cookie!"

You might wonder why Dave cared about one-third of a cookie. We had recently signed up at a workout facility nine months prior to the convention. We worked out three days a week and had committed to a special eating plan that was rather strict. Four days a week we ate mostly protein and vegetables. The fifth day was called a "free day" because we got to eat one meal consisting of anything we wanted to eat. Usually on that day we ate pasta and/or dessert. We were free to eat whatever we wanted during that one meal as long as we got right back on our eating plan the next day. Our free day for that week was the following day, and Dave had challenged me because I had eaten the piece of cookie on the wrong day.

In his own words, he was only trying to help me. But I didn't want help or advice. I wanted the cookie! I was tired, I had come a long way in the conference, and I needed something to get me to the finish line. I didn't care what it was, but it needed to be fun, pretty, or sweet. And the cookie happened to be the first thing I saw that fit that description. Being a man, Dave does not understand things like that. He is very logical and in his mind, it simply wasn't the right day to eat the cookie. He wanted me to know that I would be sorry after I ate it. However, I was not the least bit sorry. I felt that I deserved it, and in the same set of circumstances I would do it again!

My friend saw what was happening between me and Dave,

and having compassion and understanding, she put her arm around my shoulder and said, "You deserve that cookie, and if I were you, when this last session is over I would go buy a pair of shoes to go with it!" (She knows I like shoes.) She totally understood that the cookie was meeting an emotional need of mine. Being a left-brained male, Dave didn't get it at all.

I went onstage and made a joke out of it, like I usually do about most of the things that happen between Dave and me, and everyone enjoyed it immensely. Actually, the ladies cheered so long and loud and were so happy for me that I had eaten the cookie that I began to realize that there was a larger issue involved in the eating of the cookie that needed to be explored. That's how the idea for this book was birthed. Interestingly enough, when the teaching about the cookie aired on *Enjoying Everyday Life,* it was so well received that it was voted the favorite program of the year by the people who watch the broadcast. Obviously, I'd struck a nerve.

There are times when we all need to eat the cookie and buy the shoes in order to help us finish what we have started or as a way of celebrating something we have accomplished. Your cookie and shoes can be anything that you enjoy. It can be a favorite food, a nap, a manicure or pedicure. If you are a brave man reading this book, you can play golf, go fishing, go to a ballgame, or whatever helps you rest and refreshes you. You may even be a man who likes manicures, pedicures, and bubble baths, or a woman who likes to get out tools and build something amazing. We don't have to fit into some society mold. We are free to enjoy anything as long it is not immoral or illegal.

I sincerely wish that the male species was more understanding about the cookies in life, but most of them just don't seem to get it. Dave fully intended to go hit his golf balls Saturday evening, which is his way of relaxing and celebrating a job well done. But he still had the nerve to comment about my cookie! It isn't fair that cookies have calories and golf balls don't. If every golf ball Dave hit had ten calories, he would weigh a thousand pounds!

Dave truly was trying to help me when he commented on the cookie. He loves me immensely and is extremely good to me. But he simply didn't understand my need at that moment. Sadly, if we are not confident about our choices, we can easily let other peoples' comments make us feel guilty and ruin the joy we need to experience in life through doing the little things that mean a lot to us. My friend rescued me from the guilt that could have hounded me that day, and I am thankful to God for using her. I didn't need guilt as I approached the final session of the convention. I needed the cookie and the thought of shoes later that day!

> Sadly, if we are not confident about our choices, we can easily let other peoples' comments make us feel guilty and ruin the joy we need to experience in life through doing the little things that mean a lot to us.

We're Not Built for Guilt

Making people feel guilty about anything is not God's mode of operation. The source of guilt is the devil. He is the accuser of the brethren, according to the Bible (see Rev. 12:10). God will convict us of wrong choices and actions, but He never tries to make us feel guilty. Guilt presses us down and weakens us, but godly conviction brings awareness of wrong, and an opportunity to change and progress.

We are not built for guilt. God never intended His children to be loaded down with guilt, so our systems don't handle it well at all. Had God wanted us to feel guilty, He would not have sent Jesus to redeem us from guilt. He bore, or paid for, our iniquities and the guilt they cause (see Isa. 53:6 and 1 Peter 2:24–25). As believers in Jesus Christ and as sons and daughters of God, we have been set free from the power of sin (see Rom. 6:6–10). That doesn't mean that we'll never sin, but it does mean that when we do, we can admit it, receive forgiveness, and be free from guilt. Our journey with God toward right behavior and holiness is progressive, and if we have to drag the guilt from past mistakes along with us, we'll never make progress toward true freedom and joy. Perhaps this is the main reason why so few people actually enter into and enjoy the inheritance promised through relationship with Jesus Christ.

> We are not built for guilt.

Your future has no room for your past. How much time do you waste feeling guilty? It is important that you think about this, because spending time dwelling on past mistakes is something God has told us not to do. He even sent us the Holy Spirit to help us gain freedom in this area. Don't be so intense about every mistake that you make. So what if

> Your future has no room for your past. How much time do you waste feeling guilty?

you're not perfect? Nobody else is either. Besides, Jesus came for those who were sick (imperfect), not those who were well (perfect).

The Apostle Paul was very emphatic about the need to let go of past mistakes in order to have the strength to press on toward the mark of perfection that God is calling us to.

Not that I have now attained [this ideal], or have already been made perfect, but I press on to lay hold of (grasp) and make my own, that for which Christ Jesus (the Messiah) has laid hold of me and made me His own.

I do not consider, brethren, that I have captured and made it my own [yet]; but one thing I do [it is my one aspiration]: forgetting what lies behind and straining forward to what lies ahead,

I press on toward the goal to win the [supreme and heavenly] prize to which God in Christ Jesus is calling us upward.

Philippians 3:12–14

Satan will definitely try to make us feel guilty about our sins, faults, and weaknesses. Even worse, he will try to make us feel guilty when we haven't done anything wrong. Until my friend encouraged me, I was about to feel guilty about eating one third of a chocolate chip cookie on the wrong day! There was no sin in eating the cookie. We could eat a dozen cookies and it still wouldn't be sin. It would not be a good or a wise choice, but it would not be sin in the true sense of the word. I just needed a little celebration before approaching the finish of my conference, and what I almost got was a dose of guilt, frustration, and resentment—all from a teaspoonful of cookie batter!

I've surveyed many people on this subject and have found that most people feel guilty when they take the opportunity to celebrate. They push themselves to go on with no joy fuel in their tank. Joy is the fuel we need to reach the finish line of an endeavor with a good attitude. We may drive ourselves to finish, but somewhere along the way we will probably become bitter and get a chip on our shoulder if we don't lighten up and take time to celebrate the journey.

I believe that we must confront the reasons why we tend to feel guilty about enjoying and celebrating life when God has clearly ordained and commanded both. Our thinking has been warped in these areas. Satan has managed to deceive us, and by doing so he succeeds in keeping people weary and worn out, feeling resentful, and taken advantage of because of excessive work and responsibility. We need times of refreshment and recreation as well as work and accomplishment.

When I ask large audiences how many people feel guilty when they try to rest or entertain themselves or even do things they enjoy, my guess would be that at least 80 percent of the people raise their hands. I was part of that 80 percent until I decided that I was not built for guilt, and I was not going to continue allowing a renegade feeling to rule my life.

When I ask large audiences how many people feel guilty when they try to rest or entertain themselves or even do things they enjoy, my guess would be that at least 80 percent of the people raise their hands.

I studied God's word about guilt and studied His character and nature until I was totally convinced that *God is not the source of guilt*. I see guilt as an illegal alien that attacks our mind and conscience, attempting to prevent us from enjoying anything God has provided for us. Guilt has no legal right in our lives because Jesus has paid for our sins and misdeeds. If it is in us illegally, then we need to send it back where it came from—which is hell! Don't give guilt a green card or, even worse, citizenship and allow it to take up residence in you.

I was once addicted to guilt. The only time in life that I felt right was when I felt wrong. I especially had difficulty enjoying myself because I didn't feel that I deserved it. I was most definitely a person who needed to give myself permission to lighten up and not be so intense about basically everything in life. I was intense about how my children behaved and looked. I was intense about how my house looked, how I looked, and what people thought of us. I was intense about trying to change my husband into what I thought he should be. I really can't think of anything I wasn't intense about! I remember going to a doctor once because I was exhausted all the time and generally felt horrible. He talked to me five minutes and said, "You are a very intense woman and your problem is stress!" I got offended, left his office, and continued on with my intense, stressful lifestyle.

I didn't know how to trust God with daily life. I was out of balance in almost everything and I did not yet realize that celebration and enjoyment are necessary in our lives and we cannot be healthy spiritually, mentally, emotionally, or physically without them. We must remember that we are not built for guilt, and we should deal with it aggressively anytime we experience it.

The best gift you can give your family and the world is a healthy you and you cannot be healthy without celebration being a regular part of your life. You can change the entire atmosphere in your home simply by giving yourself permission to lighten up.

CHAPTER
2

Happy Birthday

I want to help you see all of the reasons you have to celebrate. Let's start with your birthday. The day you were born was an awesome day, and every anniversary of that day should be celebrated. We just celebrated our youngest grandson's first birthday, and the house was full of people, presents, and food. He couldn't have cared less, but we were having a great time! It seems we always make a big deal out of a child's first birthday, but as the years go by, we stop thinking it is important.

By the time most people reach their thirties they say things like, "It is just another day and I am just another year older." "I don't need a party, and don't worry about a gift. It's just another day." For most of my adult birthdays I have worked. The office booked a conference without realizing it was my birthday and I approved it by saying, "Oh well, it is just another birthday." People who love me send cards and gifts, and someone usually invites me out to dinner if I am in town or when I get back in town. But, I have not had a spirit of celebration in my heart about it. As far as I was concerned, I was just another year older.

I would even say things like, "When you get this old, another year doesn't matter." My attitude was wrong, and I am sorry that I missed so many chances to celebrate another year of life.

When we seriously consider what the Psalmist David said about our birth, we realize we need to celebrate the amazing work God did when He created us.

> For You did form my inward parts; You did knit me together in my mother's womb.
> I will confess and praise You for You are fearful and wonderful and for the awful wonder of my birth! Wonderful are Your works, and that my inner self knows right well.
>
> *Psalms 139:13–14*

Perhaps part of the reason why we don't feel the need to celebrate is that we lack understanding on how truly awesome we are. David said that his inner self knew that the work God had done was amazing beyond comprehension. Let's take a look at how *The Message* translates these verses.

> Oh yes, you shaped me first inside, then out;
> you formed me in my mother's womb.
> I thank you, High God—you're breathtaking!
> Body and soul, I am marvelously made!
> I worship in adoration—what a creation!
>
> *Psalms 139:13–14*

If we could see ourselves from God's perspective, we would see that we have a huge reason to celebrate the anniversary of our birth. If one year of life is worth celebrating with the gusto we had on our grandson's recent birthday, then we should celebrate even more the older we get. Why not celebrate that God kept your heart beating another year at an amazing thirty-eight million beats during the year? Your blood circulates through your body once every sixty seconds and that is really amazing considering that you have between twenty-four thousand and forty-eight thousand miles of blood vessels in your body. That means your heart pumped your blood through all those miles of vessels 525,600 times in the past year!

Our bodies are amazing vehicles. I hear my husband and sons talk in tones of wonder about some new car they admire, and yet our bodies are infinitely more finely tuned and brilliantly designed than any automobile ever made. I just passed my sixty-sixth year of life, and thanks to my new understanding of the importance of celebration, I went all out to celebrate. I decided to have a birthday week instead of a day, and I can honestly say it was the best birthday that I can remember. That was mainly due to my attitude of celebration. I realized that celebrating another year of life as a gift from God was a way of honoring Him. When I was sixty, my family gave me a wonderful huge party. But this birthday was even better, because I really celebrated with my whole heart.

I was due for some celebrating anyway. We had just been involved in several tragic situations involving people we know and love. I was drained. On top of that, I was behind in my writing schedule due to the time I had to spend on an unexpected writing project, and I needed to get started again right away on this book. My birthday just happened to be in the midst of this time and I used it as an excuse to party, relax, get some new clothes, eat, spend time with people I love, and give to others.

All of these very natural things helped me recover from the tragic events and the workload I had just had, and they helped me get ready for the next project I needed to tackle.

I tried to sit down and start this book without taking time to celebrate, and the only thing I could think to say was "Introduction"! I put that word at the top of the page and could not think of one thing to say after that. I needed to take time to refresh through celebration before creativity would flow again. I decided to have a birthday week, and for five full days I did things that I enjoyed doing. I avoided all problems, made a point of not being around people who are challenging for me to be with, and I took the time to thoroughly enjoy each thing I did. After two days of celebrating, I tried again to write and managed one sentence. After that sentence nothing else came to me. Once again I stared at the blank page on the computer and decided to celebrate a few more days! By the fifth day, I could feel in my soul that I had made a transition and was ready to work again. Today I got started at six AM and have been writing for hours. And I've enjoyed every moment of it.

I feel ready to work and be creative; in fact, I want to work! If I had denied myself the time of celebration, as I had for so many years, I would have been struggling, frustrated and resentful, thinking of how I worked all the time while other people enjoyed themselves.

I am sure that most of you women reading this book have had plenty of times when you have felt that you do all the work, nobody really appreciates you, and that your husband and children go about enjoying life without ever realizing how much you sacrifice. It is commonly called a martyr syndrome, and I had it for at least one-half of my life. The answer to the problem is not found in someone else doing something for you, although that is helpful. The real answer is you learning how to celebrate your own progress so you have strength to begin the next one without resentment. I like it when other people do things for me or encourage me, but I have decided that if they don't happen to think of it, I am going to do it myself!

Celebrate the Ordinary

Every day cannot be a birthday, and this day may be a very ordinary one for you. Perhaps you have just finished spring cleaning, and sometime before the week is over you need to visit your mom at the nursing home, take her to a doctor visit, go to the grocery store, make it to a parent-teacher conference, take little Johnnie to soccer practice, and watch your husband bowl on Friday night so he feels that you are a good wife who is interested in him. My suggestion to avoid bitterness, resentment, and perhaps a mild nervous breakdown is to take time between the spring cleaning and all the rest of the things on your schedule and do something that you really enjoy that would qualify as celebration. The first thing your mind is going to say is, "You don't have time to do that." But I am telling you that you need to take the time. And if you do, the rest of your tasks will go more smoothly and joyfully. If you don't take the time to recharge your batteries, then you are probably headed for some version of sinking emotions—discouragement, depression, despair, anger, resentment, or self-pity. When you start to feel down, just take the time to do something "up" that lifts your mood and helps you feel better about life in general.

Cleaning house is an ordinary thing, but getting the job

done can still be celebrated. Perhaps we could enjoy ordinary, everyday life more if we learned to celebrate the ordinary. I am actually inviting you to creatively find reasons to celebrate. We cannot always celebrate for days at a time like I just did for my birthday, but even small celebrations can refresh us. Eat a cookie, buy a pair of shoes, go to lunch with a good friend, sit in the sunshine, go for a walk, or put a spoonful of whipped cream in your coffee. Take the time to do whatever is special to you. It doesn't even have to take a long time, but it is necessary for optimum joy and maintaining a good attitude.

Too much of the ordinary is what we normally get bored with, but I am convinced that it's our own fault. We don't have to wait for something nice to happen to us, we can be aggressive and do something nice for ourselves. For many of you, I know this is a new thought; one that may seem foreign and even unspiritual. But I can assure you that it is part of God's plan. You can create variety, and it will keep your life more exciting. I sat with my computer on my lap for about four hours this morning and then stopped for a while to do some other things I needed to do. When I went back to my writing, I decided to sit in a different part of the house just for variety. I chose a place where I could look out the window and had plenty of light. Simple little things like this cost nothing, but they are very valuable.

> We don't have to wait for something nice to happen to us, we can be aggressive and do something nice for ourselves.

No day needs to be ordinary if we realize the gift God is giving us when He gives us another day. An extraordinary attitude can quickly turn an ordinary day into an amazing adventure. Jesus said that He came that we might have and enjoy life (see John 10:10). If we refuse to enjoy it, then it's no one's fault but our own. I would like to suggest that you take responsibility for your joy and never again give anyone else the job of keeping you happy. You can control what you do, but you cannot control what other people do. So you may be unhappy a lot of the time if you only depend on them as your source of joy. The Psalmist David said that he encouraged himself in the Lord, and if he can do it, then we can do it.

Solomon talked about celebration when he said:

Behold, what I have seen to be good and fitting is for one to eat and drink, and to find enjoyment in all the labor in which he labors under the sun all the days which God gives him—for this is his [allotted] part.

Ecclesiastes 5:18

I can see from this Scripture that the cookie was my allotted part that Saturday afternoon in 2007 at our conference. It helped me enjoy my labor, and since then I have learned a great deal about the art of celebration. I am so sorry that I lived so long without it, but I am fully committed to spending the rest of my life making up for lost time!

Every day is worth celebrating, but especially the day of your birth. Go for it and don't hold back. God has given you another year to do the ordinary and the extraordinary, and you are cheating yourself if you don't celebrate.

CHAPTER
3

You Are Worth a Little Waste

The Bible teaches us to be prudent, and that means being good managers of all of our resources. Yet there are times when God gets rather extravagant with those whom He loves. Sometimes in an effort to not be wasteful we can become downright cheap and stingy. Some people are especially that way with themselves. I know people who are generous with others, but their general attitude toward themselves is that they can do without. They say, "I don't need that," or, "I can do without that." But I believe they are depriving themselves because they don't feel worth the cost of the indulgence.

Perhaps we can learn a lesson from Jesus. He was nearing the time of His suffering and death, and He went to Simon's house, where a woman named Mary came up to Him and poured expensive perfume on His head as He was reclining at the table. Since He was at the table I am assuming that He either was or had been eating (maybe a cookie). When the disciples saw what she did, they became indignant, saying, "For what purpose is all this waste?" They talked about how the perfume could have been sold and the money given to the poor.

Jesus replied by telling them not to bother the woman because she had done a noble (praiseworthy and beautiful) thing for Him. Jesus said that they would always have the poor with them, but they would not always have Him. He said that what she had done had helped prepare Him for the trials ahead (see Matt. 26:6–12). The perfume she poured out on Jesus was probably worth about one year of wages, but her extravagance certainly blessed Him. The love she showed to Him helped give Him the strength He needed to face the upcoming days of persecution, trial, suffering, crucifixion, and death. God often works through unlikely vessels and in unusual ways to give us courage and strength. A further study of this amazing event teaches us that the home Jesus was in belonged to a leper, and the woman who blessed Him had formerly had seven demons cast out of her. It is interesting to note who Jesus chose to spend time with at this critical time in His life: it was not the religious crowd.

In this particular instance, Jesus was saying that for this time and occasion He was worth the extravagance, or what the disciples saw as waste. We know that ordinarily waste would not be good, but everything is beautiful in its time (see Eccles. 3:11). There is a time to get and a time to lose, a time to keep and a time to give away (see Eccles. 3:6). Jesus certainly believed in giving to the poor. He and His disciples kept money with them as they traveled specifically for the purpose of giving to the poor they met on their journey. But religious legalism leaves no room to be led by the Holy Spirit. Everything is controlled by rules, regulation, and laws when one is religiously legalistic. This is why Jesus had such harsh things to say to the religious people of His day. It is also the reason why, when He wanted to relax with friends, He chose ordinary people who had made mistakes and wanted forgiveness, mercy, and a better way of living.

The disciples looked at what was going on from their minds and not their hearts, and they missed the whole point. Mary had been forgiven for much and she loved Jesus very much. She loved Him so much that she was willing to take what was probably her most precious possession and pour it all over Him as an act of gratitude and worship. Her wholehearted display of affection ministered to Him in such a deep and profound way that He said it helped prepare Him for His burial. This whole story is truly amazing and contains a wonderful lesson if we really look at it deeply.

Seeing from God's View

When we look at things with the eyes of our heart we are more likely to see from God's view. The poor are certainly important, but at that moment Jesus needed to be prepared for a world-changing event and it was worth a departure from the ordinary way things were usually done.

When our ministry takes people to the mission field for the first time, they usually come home after seeing such severe poverty and feel that they should never buy anything again that is not absolutely and vitally necessary, and that they should give away everything else. We went through the same thing but soon realized that while God was asking us to help the poor, He was not asking us to become poor. People who start to feel guilty after a mission trip and begin to live on what they need to barely get by quickly become unhappy, unless of course God has given them a special grace to make such an extraordinary sacrifice. They cannot understand why they are unhappy because after all, they are doing the noble thing. However, they are doing something that is not necessary and that God never asked them to do.

We cannot labor and never enjoy the fruit of our labor. It is not in God's plan for His children. Just as we are not built for guilt, we are not destined by God to live with barely enough to get by. He is El Shaddi, the God of more than enough. He is Jehovah Jirah, the Lord our Provider. He said that He was able to do exceedingly, abundantly, above and beyond all that we could ever dare to ask, think or imagine (see Eph. 3:20). He said that if we would be faithful to bring all of our tithe into the storehouse so there would always be enough to help others, that He would open the windows of heaven and dribble out (oops, I made a mistake—He actually said POUR out) a blessing so great that we could not take it in (see Mal. 3:10).

> We cannot labor and never enjoy the fruit of our labor. It is not in God's plan for His children.

Certainly God wants and even commands us to give to others generously. You will see later in this book that in the Bible we learn that giving to the poor is part of celebrating our victories and the progress we have made in life. But God never intended that we feel guilty if we take time to enjoy the fruit of our labors. Hard work deserves reward and we must not ever think that it doesn't. God rewards those who diligently seek Him (see Heb. 11:6), so why would He not want us to enjoy the reward of other things we work diligently at?

On that Saturday afternoon in the fall of 2007, the cookie I ate part of was a reward for my hard work so far in the conference. It was to me what the sweet perfume was to Jesus. It encouraged me for the rest of the journey I needed to make. It was a principle, and to be honest, the one-third of a cookie had very little to do with it. So don't get fixated on the cookie and miss the lesson. You could start eating cookies three times a day and not get anything but fat. The cookie could easily have been a compliment from the right person, a hug, some perfume, a neck and shoulder massage, or a thousand other things, but the point was that I needed a little something for me and my emotions. We all have emotional needs, and ignoring them will cause serious problems over time. God gave us our emotions, and it is not wrong to do what is needed to keep them strong and healthy. We must not allow emotions to rule us, but denying their existence is equally dangerous.

The cookie did not fill me up. I could have done without it, it probably was a waste of calories—I know a nutritionist would say it had no food value. But I did not care at all—I WANTED THE COOKIE AND I ATE IT!

Is It Waste to Buy More of What You Already Have?

It can be a waste and a breeding ground for financial trouble to buy more of what you already have, but there are times when it is acceptable behavior. The first thing to ask yourself is if you can afford what you are purchasing. What is wasteful for one person may be totally permissible for another depending on level of income. One way to define extravagance is trying to live beyond what you can comfortably afford. I recommend that you don't buy or eat things just for entertainment or encouragement if you cannot afford it or if it will harm your overall life in some way. Everything we do should be guided by principles of wisdom.

Most women like little things like soap that smells good, perfume, earrings, shoes, a new top to wear, or some little thing that is pretty to look at. Do we need all of them? Of course we don't, but we do enjoy them. And enjoyment has intrinsic value. We need to enjoy our journey through life. My husband loves to go to the golf store and of course I can't understand that at all since he already has golf balls, clubs, gloves, shoes, hats, and all that golfing stuff. But, he loves to go there and he usually comes out with something, just like I would if I went into an accessory store for ladies.

Jesus did not die so we could be miserable and deny ourselves everything that we enjoy or that is pretty. He did say that we should deny ourselves, but He was talking about self-denial in order to serve others rather than being selfish and self-centered. Jesus did not go to the cross because we buy and wear earrings or other jewelry, or because of makeup or movies or dancing or card playing. He had to go to the cross because of jealousy, greed, anger, lust, gossip, criticism, lying, hatred, and other such sins. Obviously, there may be times when it is necessary and proper to deny ourselves the item that we already have plenty of, but we have the freedom as individuals to be led by the Holy Spirit.

I also believe there are different seasons in our lives in which we may need to follow different guidelines. When God was teaching me that I needed Him more than I needed any other "thing" in life, He told me not to ask Him for anything except more of Him until He gave me permission to do so. This was a season of self-denial in my life that lasted for six months and was for the purpose of teaching me an important spiritual lesson. We all have times like this and it is important to be able to flow in and out of the various seasons of our life comfortably. If I have to shop for earrings or Dave has to go to the golf store to be happy, then we have a problem, but if it is something we simply enjoy, then God will sanction it and even help us find what we are looking for.

The same disciples who thought Mary was being wasteful when she poured the perfume on Jesus argued among themselves over which of them they thought was the greatest. They saw and judged Mary's sacrificial gift as waste, but they failed to see their own pride, arrogance, and competitive spirit. They needed to look at themselves rather than Mary because it was their pride that was a sin, and not her generosity.

Jesus tried to tell them that they needed to clean the inside of the cup and not worry so much about the outside, but most of them never really understood what He was saying. He wanted them to realize that no matter how perfectly they behaved or how many laws and rules they kept, none of it meant anything if their hearts were not right. They never really understood that it wasn't the perfume or what it cost that was important, but it was Mary's attitude of heart that was so valuable and encouraging to Jesus. The perfume was just the vehicle that carried the love she felt and displayed.

An important lesson that I have learned is to make all of my resources available for use in the service of God and man. That doesn't mean that God will require me to give all of them away, but it does mean that I am ready to let them go if God asks me to. Occasionally God will test our obedience and loyalty to Him by asking us to give away something that means a lot to us. If we are able to obey Him promptly and with joy it is evidence that although we have things, they don't have us.

Jesus said that people who have wealth and keep on holding it will have difficulty entering the kingdom of God (see Mark 10:23). Having is not a problem, but not being able to let go of what we have is a problem. Be a channel and let what comes to you flow through you.

God Is an Amazing Decorator

Have you ever paid attention to how the temple of God was decorated under the Old Covenant? It was very beautiful and ornate, so God must like pretty things. It was built with the best wood available, and everything—and I do mean every-thing—was overlaid with gold. God's house that Solomon built to honor Him was filled with gold, silver, expensive cloth, and every kind of precious jewel known to man. It was built with the best of the best.

What we read about Heaven sounds pretty amazing, too. Streets of gold, a sea of crystal, and a gate made out of one single pearl. As someone who enjoys pretty clothes, I have noticed how the priests in the Old Testament dressed—and they were pretty decked out. My point is that God likes beautiful things, and there is nothing wrong with us liking them, too. Someone who attended one of my conferences sent a letter of complaint about me wearing rhinestone earrings. They thought the earrings were too flashy, and I couldn't help but wonder how they would feel if they made it to Heaven and saw how God decorates. Was He wasteful when He gave instructions on how the temple was to be decorated? I am sure He could have cut back on some stuff and not been so extravagant. Surely some of that gold could have been given to the poor. I think we need to understand that there are times when God is extravagant, but that doesn't mean He is being wasteful. Nothing is wasted if it is used for a right purpose, and blessing yourself at times is right and necessary.

> Nothing is wasted if it is used for a right purpose, and blessing yourself at times is right and necessary.

Religious people often say that the Apostle Paul said that women should not wear expensive clothes or jewelry and they should not have elaborate hairstyles. Some have added makeup, but I cannot find any reference to makeup in the Bible. Personally, I need mine and would suggest it for a few other people I have seen, too. If God didn't like color He would not have created it. Let's look at what Paul actually said.

Let not yours be the [merely] external adorning with [elaborate] interweaving and knotting of the hair, the wearing of jewelry or changes of clothes;
But let it be the inward adorning and beauty of the hidden person of the heart, with the incorruptible and unfading

charm of a gentle and peaceful spirit, which [is not anxious or wrought up, but] is very precious in the sight of God.

1 Peter 3:3–4

All the Apostle is saying is that women should not merely or only be concerned with how they look and having lots of clothes, but they should first and foremost be concerned with having a right heart attitude. He did not say that women shouldn't have more than one outfit and that it should be colorless and out of style. He did not say that wearing jewelry was a sin, but he did say that to be overly concerned with those things was wrong. I admit that I have seen some pretty obnoxious excess, but when I have, I have also seen obnoxious attitudes to go along with it. When people have a right heart toward God they do things in balance and are always concerned about representing God in a proper way.

God appears to me to be an awesome decorator. He can choose my wardrobe and decorate my house any time. Just look at the way He has decorated the earth. Thousands upon thousands of species of animals and birds, and trees and flowers exist. How many species of animals exist? The correct answer is that nobody really knows. Over a million have been named, but experts say there are possibly another million waiting to be discovered. There are twenty thousand species of fish, six thousand reptiles, nine thousand birds, and fifteen thousand mammals. Most don't even want to guess at the number and variety of insects on the earth. There are nearly twenty varieties of penguins—that seems a bit excessive to me, but I guess God likes variety. There are 6,500 varieties of roses, at least 7,500 varieties of apples and 7,500 varieties of tomatoes, but not all are grown commercially.

CNN.com says that research counts seventy sextillion stars within the range of modern telescopes. I am not sure how they counted them, but the point is do we need them all? Is it wasteful or excessive to have so many out there that we cannot even see them? The point I am trying to make is that God not only likes variety, He obviously has lots more of everything than He would have to have. He does exceedingly, abundantly, above and beyond what would be required. God delights in amazing us. Take the penguin for example. I love movies and documentaries about penguins. They are funny, cute, and have amazing habits. They look like they are wearing tuxedos and the way they walk is hilarious. I love the movie *Happy Feet*, which is about a penguin who could not sing like the others, but he had happy feet—he could dance! When I see penguins it makes me happy. I am convinced that God does a lot of what He does just for our enjoyment and to make us happy.

CHAPTER
4

God Likes a Party

A party is a festive occasion and would certainly qualify as a celebration. As a matter of fact many celebrations take the form of a party. We have birthday parties, Christmas parties, office parties, anniversary parties—we can make a party out of anything. The first miracle that Jesus performed that is recorded was done at a party. I think that is interesting to say the least and that it should be noted in our memory banks. Jesus was invited to a wedding and while He was there they ran out of wine so He turned some water into wine so the party could continue as planned. No matter what your particular doctrine is about wine, the fact remains that Jesus made it for the party, so don't get caught up in the wine and miss the point. Jesus attended the party, He had nothing against the party, and He wanted the people to enjoy the party.

I am making a big deal out of this because I believe that many religious people could not have a good time at a party if their lives depended on it. They would probably find something wrong with the music, the way people dressed and, of course, the wine. They would think the money spent to have the party could have been used for a more important purpose. Religious people just do not seem to know how to have a really good time, but people who have a genuine relationship with Jesus can somehow enjoy everything. The religious person tends to avoid almost everything that could be considered fun in an effort not to sin, but the person who has close fellowship with God and is led by the Holy Spirit can do all things in moderation.

During my first few years as a Christian I went to church and tried to be good to a point, but was definitely a middle-of-the-road, compromising Christian. Then I came to a place in life where I wanted more of God than I had, and I got really serious about my relationship with Him. I got so serious that all I did was go to church, prayer meeting, and Bible studies. I did not go to parties! I was much too serious-minded about God to waste my time on frivolous things like that. I stopped playing volleyball, I stopped bowling, I stopped playing golf with Dave—as a matter of fact I stopped everything that was fun and became dangerously close to being one of the Pharisees that Jesus had disdain for (see Matt. 23). I finally got spiritual burnout, and my life was so out of balance and boring that I began to search the Scriptures for myself about joy and the enjoyment of life. I discovered that God likes parties, a playful attitude, laughter, celebration, and festivals. He also likes holiness, and the good news is we can be holy and enjoy a party. Jesus actually said that He came so we could have and enjoy life and have it in abundance until it overflows. I sure didn't have that, so I decided I was going to learn to really enjoy life. I was definitely one of the people that I am writing this book for. I needed to give myself permission to lighten up!

I know some of the more religious-minded people are thinking right now, "Well Joyce, the Bible does say to be serious-
minded, sober, disciplined, prudent, and diligent." They are
correct and we need to be all of those things, but we also need
to celebrate, and if we don't we will be missing the spice in life.
Everything, including us, will be tasteless and boring.

Join My Party

When Jesus invited people to become His disciples and follow
Him, He asked them if they wanted to join His party. I realize
He was talking about His group, but I like to think that traveling with Jesus was probably a lot of fun as well as a lot of hard
work. He told the rich young ruler that we read about in Luke
18 to lay aside his selfish lifestyle and join His party. The rich
young ruler had money, but it controlled him, and Jesus wanted
him to learn that real joy was not found in what we own, but
living for the right purpose. Repeatedly throughout the gospels
(Matthew, Mark, Luke, and John) we see Jesus invited people to
leave their lifestyles and side with His party, and He is still issu-
ing that invitation today.

Living for God, serving Him and others, can be a blast if we
look at it with the mind of Christ. I am working all day today
and I can either look at it as w-o-r-k, or I can decide I am going
to have a party (fun) while I do my work. It comes down to
a-t-t-i-t-u-d-e! What will my attitude be? The mission that Jesus
had could not have been any more serious and yet I am positive that He laughed with His disciples, made jokes about their
goofy ways, enjoyed food, rested, and somehow managed to

turn the mission into something that was enjoyable. When we receive Jesus Christ as our Savior and decide we want to be a Christian and live a Christian lifestyle we are not going to a solemn assembly or a funeral, we are joining His party! My favorite image of Jesus is one I have seen of Him laughing.

Jesus can even make dying to self, which means being delivered from selfish, self-centered living, an interesting journey if we look at it properly. I speak a lot on spiritual maturity, dying to selfishness, taking up our cross and living holy lives, and I am continually amazed at how much people laugh while I do it. Somehow the Holy Spirit brings the teaching out of me in a way that makes people laugh while they are being corrected. God is amazing! People tell me all the time how funny I am and yet I speak a very straightforward, hard-hitting message that is quite serious. I have joined Jesus' party!

You Are Invited to the Party

One of the most well known and loved Bible stories is about a young man who left his father's house to go out into the world and live life his own way. He wasted all of his inheritance in undisciplined living and finally ended up with a job feeding hogs and eating what they ate. He made the brilliant decision to return home to his father's house realizing that he would have a better life as a servant with his father than living the way he was living in the world. His father saw him coming as he looked into the distance and immediately planned a party. The exact words he spoke were, "Let us revel and feast and be happy and make merry" (Luke 15:23). He got his son new clothes, a special ring, and new shoes, and he prepared an amazing feast. He was extremely happy that his son had come to his right mind and had returned home. Everyone was enjoying the party, the music was loud, and the older son who was returning from working in the field heard it. He asked what was going on and when he heard the news he became indignant and angry and refused to go to the party. His father pleaded with him, but he preferred to sulk, feel sorry for himself, and make accusations toward his brother and father. None of his bad attitude prompted his father to stop the party, but it did keep him from entering in.

The older brother reminded his father that he had served and worked for him many years and never caused any trouble, and not once had anyone given him a party. His father replied that he could have had a party anytime he wanted one, because everything the father had was always his. To me, this is a most amazing lesson and one that we cannot afford to miss seeing. God loves us, and all that He has is ours as long as we belong to Him. He appreciates our work and effort to please Him, but

> Every day can be a party if we learn the art of celebration.

if we refuse to enjoy the benefits of being a child of God that is our fault, not His. We can have a party any time we want one. Every day can be a party if we learn the art of celebration.

Jesus said that the kingdom of Heaven is like a king who gave a wedding banquet for his son, and he sent his servants to summons those who had been invited but they refused to come. He sent other servants and tried once again to get them to come to the banquet (party) but they treated it with contempt and each went away to his farm or business (see Matt. 22:2–5). It is very sad to me that so many people live a life of stress and pressure because they simply don't know the art and value of enjoying the journey.

Feasts and Festivals

When I study the Old Testament and the lifestyle of the Israelites, who were God's chosen people, I see that it was filled with parties. The first celebration we see recorded in biblical history is the Sabbath, which was a celebration of creation. God worked six days, and on the seventh day He rested from His labors and took time to enjoy what He had accomplished. He commanded that the seventh day of each week be celebrated as a day holy to the Lord. The Sabbath was a day when people would remember and celebrate all that He had done for them, and what He had created (see Exod. 20:8–11). It was a time of reflection, restoration, and celebration.

The Passover feast and celebration was instituted for people to always remember how God had protected and delivered them from the angel of death that passed through Egypt, killing all of the firstborn animals and people (see Lev. 23:5). The slaying of the firstborn was a judgment on Pharoah who had refused to obey God and let the Israelites go from their slavery in Egypt.

This night was a night to remember, and it deserved a yearly celebration. God wants us to remember what He has done for us. If you are not Jewish you probably don't celebrate Passover, but we should keep the spirit of that feast by celebrating similar things that God has done for us. We should call them to mind, discuss them with friends and family, and never stop celebrating the goodness of God in our lives.

The Feast of Unleavened Bread began immediately following the Passover feast and lasted seven days. It was instituted to remind people of their exodus from Egypt and that they had left the old life behind and were entering a new way of living. Just imagine—they had one party right after another (see Lev. 23:6–8).

The Feast of Firstfruits came next. It was a celebration at the time of the barley harvest to remind the people how God had provided for them (see Lev. 23:9–14). This feast lasted one day.

The Feast of Pentecost came at the end of barley harvest and the beginning of wheat harvest and showed joy and thanksgiving over the bountiful harvest. This feast also lasted one day.

The Feast of Trumpets was next, and it was a one-day feast expressing joy and thanksgiving to God. Part of this celebration was the blowing of trumpets (see Lev. 23:23–25).

The Day of Atonement was a big day (see Lev. 23:26–32), a day when sin was removed from the people and the nation and fellowship was restored with God. It was a day when the people were required to afflict themselves with fasting, penitence, and humility. I am glad as New Covenant Christians we can have this celebration *continually* rather than once a year. I am also glad that Jesus humbled and afflicted Himself on our behalf and we can celebrate what He has done.

If we [freely] admit that we have sinned and confess our sins, He is faithful and just (true to His own nature and promises) and will forgive our sins [dismiss our lawlessness] and [*continuously*] (emphasis mine) cleanse us from all unrighteousness [everything not in conformity to His will in purpose, thought, and action].

1 John 1:9

The Feast of Tabernacles lasted seven days and was a celebration of God's protection and guidance in the desert as the Israelites traveled from Egypt to the Promised Land. It renewed Israel's commitment to God as well as their trust in His guidance and protection (see Lev. 23:33–43).

The Israelites also had a habit of celebrating after a job well done. In Ezra 6:14–16 we see that the people celebrated the finishing and dedication of the house they had built for God. They celebrated weddings and probably birthdays and anniversaries. They had a party when their children came of age called bar mitzvah. Truthfully, it seems to me that they used any excuse they could to celebrate and that the celebrations were not only sanctioned by God, they were ordered and ordained by Him.

Are you beginning to catch my drift? God definitely likes a party!

CHAPTER
5

Celebrate Your Progress

Our youngest grandson recently stood alone for the first time. We were out of town on this joyous occasion, but we received a phone call telling us the great news. I vividly remember that there were four adults in the car when we received the news and three of us acted fairly ridiculously about the event. I actually clapped my hands together. Dave grinned from ear to ear and in a very surprised tone said, "REALLY!" A good friend was also in the car and she got excited. I heard questions like, "How long did he stand there?" and "Has he done it more than once?" Nobody asked if he sat down again, although we all knew that he did. We were even aware that he could have fallen down, but we did not care about anything other than his progress. We had a similar scene at our house when he smiled for the first time, ate his first solid food, crawled, and said "mama" and "da-da." We get really excited about any little progress that he makes and we all express it to him to encourage him. Dave and I just spent several days with the baby, and, to be honest, we probably encouraged him hundreds of times during those few days.

I don't remember even one time that we chastised him for what he could not do yet.

When I am out of town and call my son and daughter-in-law, I always ask if Travis has done anything new. My daughter-in-law sends me pictures of new things, like him in his swimming pool, on his swing, or standing at his play table. God used this example to help me understand that He celebrates our progress just like we celebrate the progress of our children and grandchildren. We celebrate our dog's progress by giving her treats. We even have some that are in the shape of a cookie! If we can take time to make an effort to celebrate the dog going potty outside, then surely we can find time to celebrate our own progress. Celebration strengthens us. In fact, I believe that if we don't celebrate occasions of progress, we are weakened and experience unnecessary defeat.

Our dog was staying with a friend while we were out of town, and she told me that even though she was taking Duchess out to go potty, she would come in, look at her, squat in front of her and tinkle on the floor. I was shocked and could not understand it until I asked if they were giving her treats after she did her job outside. They were not giving them to her, and she was letting them know that if they were not going to celebrate her progress and give her a treat, then she would make a real mess for them to deal with. Perhaps we are the same way—if we don't get our treats we display bad behavior!

God isn't keeping a record of each time we fall, but He is excited about our progress, and we should be excited, too! I spent way too many years mourning over my faults and weaknesses. I was taught to grieve over my sin, but nobody in the church world ever told me to celebrate my progress, and I think that is tragic. If you have missed this important lesson like I did, then today I am telling you to celebrate, celebrate, and then celebrate your progress some more.

God isn't keeping a record of each time we fall, but He is excited about our progress, and we should be excited, too!

I am not where I want to be in terms of holy behavior, but thank God I am not where I used to be. I have made a lot of progress in the thirty-three years that I have had a serious relationship with God. God has changed me so much that truly I am a new creature just as His word promises in 2 Corinthians 5:17. My husband probably thinks he has been married to several women during his journey with me, because I certainly am not like the one he started with. Change and progress are beautiful. They are a sign that we are alive and God is working! We need to celebrate progress.

The Bible discusses rejoicing 170 times, and if we study the word we find it is an emotion that needs an outward expression. We may clap our hands like I did when I heard about my grandson's progress, we might shout as Dave did when our last son was born and he had the privilege of being in the delivery room, or we might go get a pedicure because we are rejoicing over and celebrating the fact that we have not wasted a day in self-pity for three months. If you are really rejoicing, you might even eat a cookie while you get the pedicure!

The Bible says that the path of the righteous grows brighter and brighter every day (Prov. 4:18). If you can look back and say, "I've improved over the last year. My behavior is a little bit better. I'm a little more patient. I'm more giving. I'm a tiny bit less selfish. Then you can celebrate! If you feel you have made no progress at all then the devil is probably lying to you. He has a bad habit of reminding us daily of how far we still have to go. I have noticed that the devil is not very encouraging or complimentary and that listening to him is very counterproductive. If you are reading this book it means that you want to improve and the truth is that anyone who wants to improve will improve. Your path is growing brighter and clearer every day and celebrating our progress is one of the ways we say "Thank You" to God.

Last night I lost my temper over the remote control for the television. I had worked hard all day on this book and finally got all settled in to watch a movie. When I turned the television on I noticed that the remote control was flashing "low battery." It had just enough battery power to turn the television on, but then it went dead and wouldn't even so much as turn it off. The volume had come on really loud, and I couldn't turn it down. I called for Dave and although he was almost in the shower, he heard the panic in my voice and decided to get dressed and to try to rescue me. We thought it would be an easy fix. We would simply put new batteries in the remote, but we only had three batteries and it required four. My creative side kicked in and I suggested that we take the batteries out of a remote for one of the other televisions in the house and use them in the remote for the one we wanted to watch that evening (it had a bigger screen).

We got all the batteries on the coffee table and of course neither one of us can see without our glasses on. We got our glasses, but for some reason we were not seeing well even with them. The light was dim in the room, but being a male and unwilling to admit that he could not see, Dave continued to put the batteries in, first one way and then another, without success. By this time, neither of the remote controls worked. The batteries were spread out on the coffee table, and we probably had the good ones mixed up with the bad ones. At this point in our journey I wanted to try to fix them myself. Dave wouldn't give them to me, and I was getting angrier by the second. As we went to the sliding glass door so hopefully we could see better with outside light, from a leaned-over position we both raised up at the same time and Dave's hard head hit mine. I sounded as if I had lost my salvation for a few seconds.

Of course as soon as I calmed down I felt bad that I'd lost my temper, but since I now know that I am not built for guilt I had to resolve the situation. I admitted my mistake, asked God to forgive me and tried to think of how I was going to celebrate this mess. I suddenly realized that although I could not celebrate losing my temper, I could celebrate the fact that I was forgiven!

Years ago I would have felt guilty for days before I finally crawled out of the pit of despair and would have been sure that God was terribly disappointed with me. Now I know that nothing I do surprises Him! He knew all about me before I was ever born and still wants a relationship with me. He feels the same way about you. I strongly imagine that Jesus had a good laugh last night as He watched Dave and me try to fix the remote controls. We are often like a modern version of Lucille Ball and Desi Arnaz from *I Love Lucy*. If God recorded anything from last night, I am sure it was the fact that I have grown to the point that I don't waste time mourning over something that Jesus made provision for on the cross, which is our sins.

Find ways to celebrate your progress instead of mourning excessively over your mistakes. I am not suggesting that we don't take our sins seriously because we should, but let's also celebrate God's mercy and forgiveness.

The morning after the television remote fiasco I had another interesting challenge. I needed a certain makeup brush that I knew I had used the previous day. I rummaged through my makeup and could not find it, so I got up and took everything out of the container one thing at a time and still could not find it. I knew for sure that I used it the day before. I searched the drawer, another box, the cabinet under the sink, and finally took a deep breath and used a different brush. As soon as I had finished applying all of my makeup and had my hair fixed, I found the brush. It was a black brush and the counter top on the sink is also black, so it had been right in front of me all the time but I did not see it.

The reason I bring this up is because although it was frustrating, I didn't get upset about it as I had done the night before with the other situation. I believe if I had spent the evening condemning myself because I'd gotten angry, then I probably would have gotten angry again the next day. Condemnation weakens us and we keep repeating the same error over and over, but celebration strengthens us. You may remember that I had chosen to celebrate the fact that I was forgiven, and as I said I believe it helped me resist the temptation to get angry the next time I was confronted with something ridiculous that was just stealing my time. The devil doesn't like a party or any kind of authentic joy or celebration, so perhaps if we learn to do it more, we will hear less from him.

Punishment or Reward

How can you motivate yourself to do the things you know you need to do? Is it better to reward yourself for doing well and making progress, or to punish yourself when you make mistakes or do not reach your expectations? I believe experience teaches us that rewarding ourselves for a job well done is always better than punishment.

I have set some goals for myself at the gym for this year. I want to move up in the amount of weight I can bench press and I also want to be able to do lunges in such a manner that my knee touches the floor during the exercise. If you don't know what either of these exercises are, let me just say that for a woman my age who did not begin exercising until two years ago, they both mean pain!

I reached my goal on the bench press within a month after setting it, but I have not been able yet to reach my goal with the lunges. Suppose I decide to punish myself for not reaching the one goal by denying myself the privilege of eating dessert for two weeks, but I do nothing to reward myself for the other goal I did reach. Experience teaches us that I would begin to connect the lunges with punishment and would more than likely begin to dread and despise the lunges. I might even lower my goal so I could remove the punishment.

On the other hand, if I continued to try to reach my goal concerning lunges, but rewarded myself in some way for reaching my goal with bench presses, I would try harder to reach my other goal because I would mentally connect goal-reaching with reward. I already know that I am going to reward myself and celebrate after I finish this book, and knowing that makes it easier for me to keep working.

As parents we are often tempted to punish our children for what they do wrong, yet we fail to notice and reward what they do right. I think we should make a big deal out of our children's strong points and downplay their weaknesses. I remember getting in trouble a lot while I was growing up, but I honestly don't remember much encouragement. I do remember my father telling me that I would never amount to anything. Nobody ever told me I could do anything I set my mind to, or that I had God-given abilities that I needed to develop. I left home at age eighteen with a determination to prove to the world and myself that I had value and ability, but I went about it the wrong way. I became a workaholic who had never learned how to value reward and enjoyment.

I recently saw a movie about a child whose mom was a severe perfectionist, and no matter what kind of work the child brought home from school the mom always found something that could have and should have been done better. She never mentioned what the child did well. Of course, the girl felt so discouraged that her grades began sliding downhill. However, she got a new teacher who was a very positive lady who knew how to motivate children. She immediately saw that the child needed encouragement and began to give it to her in generous proportions. Each thing the child did a good job with was complimented in writing on her papers. For example, instead of saying, "You spelled two words wrong," she said, "Your handwriting is beautiful and your story is great. Your spelling can improve a little, but we will work on that together." You guessed it—the child loved the teacher and began to improve dramatically because she responded better to reward than she did to punishment.

I find that rewarding myself even in small ways motivates me. It gives me something to look forward to while I am doing the job that needs to be done. As I write this book I set goals for myself each day of how much I want to finish, and as I reach that goal I stop and do something that I enjoy. I go to a little restaurant in town that I really enjoy and sit out on the patio and eat, or I make a latte for myself and take a break, or I go get a massage. I could name a dozen things, but I think you get the point. What I enjoy may be different than what you enjoy, but you need to reward yourself as you work toward reaching your goals. Yesterday I worked longer than usual and I already know in my heart that today I need to work a little less and do something I enjoy so I don't get too weary of just writing and writing and writing. I refuse to be a driven person who is afraid to follow my heart.

Celebrate Change

As children of God we need to be committed to change. Throughout our journey here on earth God's Spirit will be working with and in us, helping us change for the better. In order to make progress we need to see what we are doing wrong, and be willing to learn better ways to do it. God wants us to see truth (reality) so we can agree with Him that change is needed, but we don't need to punish ourselves when we see our faults or to feel guilty and condemned. We can even learn to celebrate the changes that need to be made in us and our lives.

When Jesus ascended to Heaven He sent the Holy Spirit to help us make progress in holy behavior. The Holy Spirit works holiness in us, and He does it through convicting us of wrong behavior and convincing us to do things God's way. He not only shows us what needs to change, He also gives us the strength to change. He is our Strengthener! John 16:7–13 gives us understanding of the ministry of the Holy Spirit in our lives. He is our Comforter, Counselor, Teacher, Helper, Advocate, Intercessor, Strengthener, and Standby. He lives in close fellowship with us. That means He is always present and His goal is to help us be what God wants us to be so we can enjoy what God wants us to enjoy. Every believer's life should bring glory to God, and that requires an attitude that says, "Change me and make me what you want me to be."

Change and growth is a process that will continue as long as we are on earth in our human bodies. Progress is vitally important, but perfection is impossible. We can have perfect hearts toward God and His plan for us, but our behavior will always be lacking perfection in one way or another.

> Progress is vitally important, but perfection is impossible.

You, therefore, must be perfect [growing into complete maturity, having reached the proper height of virtue and integrity], as your heavenly Father is perfect.

Matthew 5:48

We can see from this Scripture that perfection means growing! I am of the opinion that as long as we are cooperating with the Holy Spirit to the best of our ability, and we sincerely want to change, God counts us as perfect in Christ while we make the journey.

Conviction is the tool the Holy Spirit uses to let us know we are doing something wrong. We sense inside of us that our actions, words, or attitudes are wrong. What should our attitude be toward this conviction? I think it needs to be a joyful attitude.

Those whom I [dearly and tenderly] love, I tell their faults and convict and convince and reprove and chasten [I discipline and instruct them]. So be enthusiastic and in earnest and burning with zeal and repent [changing your mind and attitude].

Revelation 3:19

God views conviction, correction, and discipline as something to be celebrated rather than something to make us sad or frustrated. Why should we celebrate when God shows us that something is wrong with us? Enthusiasm sounds like a strange response, but in reality the fact that we can see something that we were once blind to is good news. For many years of my life I was able to be rude, insensitive, and selfish and not even know it. I had a master's degree in manipulation, but actually had myself convinced that I was only trying to help people do what was right. Of course I did not see the pride I had that caused me to think *my* way was always the right way. I was greedy, envious, and jealous but I did not see any of it. That is a sad condition to be in, but people who have no relationship with Jesus and who do not study God's word are blind and deaf in the spiritual sense.

My heart was hard from years of being hurt by people, harboring bitterness, and doing things my own way. When our heart is hard we are not sensitive to the touch of God. When He convicts us we don't feel it. Therefore, when we make enough progress in our relationship with God that we begin to sense when we are doing something wrong, that is good news. It is a sign of progress and should be celebrated joyfully. The longer we serve God and study His ways the more sensitive we become. We eventually grow to the place where we know immediately when we are saying or doing something that is not pleasing to God and we have the option of repenting and making a fresh start.

My response to conviction used to be immediately coming under condemnation. Condemnation presses us down and weakens us, it makes us feel guilty and miserable, but conviction is intended to lift us out of a fault. The Holy Spirit shows us our fault, and then helps us overcome it. When God's conviction quickly turned into guilt for me I dreaded it and my attitude was, "Great! Another thing wrong with me that I have to try to fix." I did not understand the process at all; so due to lack of knowledge on my part, the devil was able to take the things God meant for my good and turn them into torment. How do you respond when you are convicted by the Holy Spirit that you are doing something wrong? Do you feel bad and guilty, or do you realize that the very fact that you can feel God's conviction is good news? It means that you are alive to God and growing spiritually.

I believe we should be thankful when God convicts us, and we truly should celebrate the fact that we have seen something that will help us change and be able to glorify God more. Each time you are convicted of sin, try lifting your hands in praise and saying, "Thank You, God, that You love me enough not to leave me alone in my sin. Thank You that I can feel Your displeasure when I sin. Thank You for changing me into what You want me to be." This kind of attitude will open the way for you to make progress rather than being stuck in your sin due to being blind to it, or through condemnation from the devil.

When God shows us a fault He does not expect us to fix it. He only wants us to acknowledge it, to agree with Him, to be sorry for it, and to be willing to turn away from it. He knows— and we need to know—that we cannot change ourselves, but He will change us if we study His word and cooperate with His Holy Spirit.

Change of all types is worth celebrating because it is required for progress. The process may not bring joy, but later on it will produce the peaceable fruit of righteousness that God desires and that we can enjoy (see Heb. 12:11). Give yourself permission to lighten up and don't be so intense about your own perfection. Do your best and let God do the rest. As long as you are making progress God is pleased.

CHAPTER
6

Celebrate through Giving

Throughout the Bible we see people celebrating progress and victory in a variety of ways. One of those ways was to specifically take the time to give an offering to God and to thank Him.

Noah had been in the ark one year and ten days when God told him it was time to go forth and begin a new life. I cannot even imagine how happy he and his family (and the animals) were to see dry ground and have their feet on solid soil. The first thing that Noah did was to build an altar to the Lord and sacrifice various animals to Him. In Noah's day this was the acceptable method of giving to God and showing appreciation for what He had done. God was pleased when He smelled the pleasant odor and He pronounced a blessing on Noah and his sons and said to them, "Be fruitful and multiply and fill the earth" (Gen. 9:1).

We would quickly add a lot of celebration time to our lives if we would take the time to give thanks and perhaps some other type of offering when God does amazing things for us. An attitude of gratitude shows a lot about the character of a person. We should never have an attitude of entitlement, but we should have one that says, "I know I don't deserve God's goodness, but I am sure grateful for it."

> An attitude of gratitude shows a lot about the character of a person.

Abram (later renamed Abraham) regularly built altars to God and sacrificed, giving praise and thanks to God for his progress as he journeyed through the land. God had asked Abram to leave everything he was familiar with, including home and family, and go to a place that would be shown to him as he went. I cannot even imagine the difficulty of obeying such a request. Leave everything! Go where? What for? Abram found the courage to go and throughout his journey he took time to celebrate the progress he had made so far (see Gen. 12:7–8, 13:4). God was leading him, taking care of him and keeping him safe. Surely at the end of each day we should take time to celebrate in our hearts that God has kept us safe and enabled us to do whatever needed to be done. The evening meal could be used as a point of contact for this type of celebration. The feasts of Israel usually included food, so why not turn an ordinary dinner into a celebration? It won't take any special preparation; all you will need is a heart full of thanksgiving and a willingness to take a few moments and express it to God.

It is easy for us to get caught up in looking at how far we have to go in reaching our goals instead of celebrating how far we have come. Think about it. How far have you come since you became a Christian? How much have you changed? How much happier are you? Are you more peaceful than you were before? Do you have hope? There is always plenty to celebrate if we look for it.

> It is easy for us to get caught up in looking at how far we have to go in reaching our goals instead of celebrating how far we have come.

A thorough study of the Bible shows us that the men and women who God used in mighty ways always had the attitude of celebrating what God had done. They did not take His goodness for granted, but they openly showed appreciation for little things as well as big ones.

God Parted the Red Sea

Have you ever had a time when you felt that your back was against the wall? You had a big problem and no solution, and then suddenly God did something amazing and enabled you to escape safely from your problem. Most of us can think of a time like that. When the Israelites were led out of Egypt by God working through Moses, they eventually found themselves in a very distressing situation. The Red Sea was in front of them and the Egyptian army was behind them. They had no place to go; they were trapped! God had promised their deliverance, and what He did was amazing indeed. He actually parted the Red Sea and the Israelites walked across on dry ground, but as the Egyptian army followed, the sea closed up over them and they drowned.

When the Israelites reached the other side, the first thing they did was start to celebrate. They sang a song that came straight from their hearts, recorded in nineteen verses in the Bible (see Exod. 15:1–19). After the song, two of the women took out a type of tambourine, and all the women followed them with their tambourines and they danced and sang some more. The entire song talked of what God had done, how great He was, how He had redeemed them and dealt with their enemies. We would probably experience more victory in life if we would take time to celebrate the ones we have already had. Once again, it is operating on the principle of being grateful for what we have instead of taking an inventory of what we do not have yet.

God Rebuilds the Broken-down

Many of us are in a broken-down condition when we finally humble ourselves and ask God to do His work in us. God is a builder and a restorer of what was once lost and destroyed. I had lost my innocence through abuse, I had no confidence, was filled with shame, guilt, bitterness, and many other painful emotions. But, God! I love that phrase which is found in God's word. But, God—worked in my life and has rebuilt and restored what was once broken down and useless. History is filled with records of people who can tell a similar story.

Nehemiah and his kinsmen (the Jews) who had escaped exile lived in pitiful conditions. The wall of their city was broken down, and for any town in those times that was a dangerous thing. Their wall was their protection from the surrounding enemies who seemed to be everywhere.

Nehemiah was told of the terrible condition his kinsmen lived in and, after weeping, fasting, and praying for days, he went to the king and asked for permission and timber to rebuild the temple gate, the city wall, and a house for himself to live in. Nehemiah was a man of action. When he saw a need or an injustice he wanted to do something about it, and we should be the same way. I think it is interesting that he asked to help the people and he was willing to work hard, but he also asked for a house for himself. Perhaps he realized that by the time he got the project finished he would need a nice place in which to live and relax.

The project was a huge one, and it took a long time and a lot of determination. During the rebuilding Nehemiah and the other workers experienced constant opposition from their enemies who tried to prevent them from building by distracting them. However, persistence paid off and eventually the project was completed. One of the first things they did after they reached their goal was to celebrate! Ezra the priest told the people, "Go your way, eat the fat, drink the sweet drink, and send portions to him for whom nothing is prepared; for this day is holy to our Lord. And be not grieved and depressed, for the joy of the Lord is your strength and stronghold" (Neh. 8:10).

Notice that the priest told them to rejoice. It was the right thing to do spiritually. The party was sanctioned by God or, even better, it was commanded by God. Just imagine God told them to eat fat and sugar! Sounds like a cookie day to me! They needed to celebrate a good job well done. Celebration is part of our recovery. It revives us for the next project or job we have to do. Do you take time to celebrate when you finish a project, or do you merely begin the next one? If you don't reward yourself in some way for your hard work you are missing out on part of God's plan. Remember, He rewards those who are diligent (see Heb. 11:6).

God not only told them to enjoy themselves, but He told them to send portions to those who were in need. I have learned over the past few years through studying God's love that giving to others is one of the ways we can and should celebrate our own victories. It is a way of saying, "I sure am happy about what God has done for me, and I want to reach out and make someone else happy."

Esther was used by God to bring deliverance to the Jews. A wicked man named Haman had a plot to destroy them—but, God! God had his own plan and it was a plan for deliverance. He used Esther and her uncle Mordecai to bring this wicked plan to the attention of the king and through them God achieved deliverance for the Jews. When the victory had been won the Jews gathered together to celebrate. They needed it and God wanted them to have it. Mordecai recorded the things that had taken place because it was part of the Jewish history that needed to be passed on to their descendants. He also commanded that the Jews keep the fourteenth and fifteenth day of the month of Adar, the days of their victory, yearly as a time of celebration and remembering what God had done. They were instructed to remember that their sorrow had been turned into gladness and "from mourning into a holiday—that they should make them days of feasting and gladness, days of sending choice portions to one another and gifts to the poor" (Esther 9:22).

Giving is a central part of the Christian lifestyle and we should do it aggressively and with joy. God has given us His Son Jesus as the best gift He could give and in Jesus we have all other things. In Him we have been blessed with every spiritual blessing in the heavenly realm (see Eph. 1:3).

It is the will of God that we give thanks at all times and in everything (see 1 Thess. 5:18). Thanksgiving must have an expression in order to be complete. We can say that we are thankful, but do we show it? Are we expressing it? We say "thank you," but there are other ways of showing appreciation and one of them is giving to people who have less than we do. Giving to the poor is commanded by God. It is one of the ways we can keep a continual cycle of blessing operating in our lives. God gives to us and we show appreciation by giving to someone else, and then He blesses us some more so we can do it all over again.

The Bible puts it plainly. When God blesses you as He promised, find a poor man and give to him. Do not harden your heart, but open your hands wide to your brethren. If you give to him freely without begrudging it then the Lord will bless you in all your work and all that you undertake (see Deut. 15:6–8, 15:10). What we give to others as a result of obedience to God is never lost. It leaves our hand temporarily, but it never leaves our life. We give it, God uses it to bless someone else, and then He returns it to us multiplied. I like the way God does things, don't you?

> What we give to others as a result of obedience to God is never lost. It leaves our hand temporarily, but it never leaves our life.

Altars and Memorials

Under the Old Covenant, men and women of God regularly built altars and sacrificed animals or grain on them as an outward sign of their inward gratitude. As we have seen, they frequently established yearly holidays that were to commemorate and bring to remembrance something wonderful God had done for them. The Bible has 396 references to altars. We find them mentioned from Genesis to Revelation. They have historically always been a part of worship, praise, and thanksgiving, and they will even be in Heaven, according to what the Apostle John saw and recorded in the book of Revelation.

We also find several references to memorials. These were altars or buildings or permanent objects that served as reminders. They could also be a day or days set aside yearly for the purpose of remembering. Altars and memorials are solid objects that give substance to our show of thankfulness. People often build some type of memorial as an object that will stand as a reminder of their lost loved ones. We put tombstones on graves as memorials. We give awards, plaques, and trophies, which are objects that help us remember our victories. We are spiritual beings, but we also have souls and bodies and we need to have tangible objects as references to remind us of things.

Another thing the Israelites did was to write things down as a memorial to what God had done. I have kept a journal of the challenges in my life and the victories for thirty-three years. The Bible that we love and base our life on is a memorial to what God has done for us. When we see our Bible it immediately says all kinds of things to us. We may not take the time to think through all of them, but oddly enough the presence of a Bible can give comfort even to people who don't know one word that is in it. The Bible reminds us that God exists and has something to say to us. Have you ever made a notation in your Bible next to a verse that spoke to you during a particular time of challenge or joy? As I leaf through my Bible, I see notes in the margins, sometimes accompanied by the date, and I remember exactly what I was going through when that verse spoke to me. As I reread it, I'm visiting the memorial of a moment in time when God moved me in a special way.

I firmly believe that saying "thank you" is good, but doing something tangible, at least part of the time, is even better.

Enter into His gates with thanksgiving and a thank offering and into His courts with praise! Be thankful and say so to Him, bless and affectionately praise His name!

Psalm 100:4

Please notice that the Psalmist suggested we come with thanksgiving (words) and a thank offering (something tangible). When we come together in church to worship, giving is part of our worship. It is a tangible way of saying, "God, I really appreciate all that you have done for me." Giving is a way to celebrate the goodness of God. Why not make a decision to be more generous than you have ever been in your life? You cannot outgive God because He will take your gift, bless someone with it, and bring it back to you multiplied. What you give may be gone temporarily, but it never leaves your life. Giving brings joy to us and blessing to others.

CHAPTER
7

A Time to Remember

I have often said that I think we forget what we should remember and remember what we should forget. Jesus chastised the disciples on one of their journeys because they had forgotten about a miracle He had done. They had started out on a trip and suddenly remembered that they had forgotten to bring enough bread. They only had one loaf and that would not be nearly enough. In a short while Jesus began to teach the disciples to beware of, and on their guard concerning, the leaven of the Pharisees and Herod. Jesus of course was talking about being on their guard against deception, but the disciples reasoned among themselves that He was talking about the fact that they had forgotten to bring bread, as if that would have concerned Jesus at all. He then began to chastise them, asking if they had forgotten when He fed five thousand people with five loaves of bread. Had they forgotten another amazing miracle when He fed four thousand with seven loaves? Had they remembered, they would not be worried about going hungry because of not having brought enough bread with them.

If we would remember the miracles God has done in our past we would not so easily fall into worry and fear when we have new challenges to face. When David was facing Goliath and nobody was encouraging him, he remembered the lion and the bear that he had already slain with God's help. Because of remembering the past, he had no fear of the current situation.

> If we would remember the miracles God has done in our past we would not so easily fall into worry and fear when we have new challenges to face.

Are you facing something right now that looms before you like a giant in your life? Is it illness or financial lack? Is it relationship problems? Is it something you have never done before and you don't know where to begin? The truth is that it doesn't matter what it is because nothing is impossible for God. Take some time right now and recall some of the things He has helped you with and brought you through in the past. Think about and talk about those things and you will find courage filling your heart.

> Are you facing something right now that looms before you like a giant in your life?

I was abused for approximately fifteen years; my first husband abandoned me when I was pregnant and he lived with another woman. I had breast cancer in 1989; I had to have a hysterectomy; I suffered with migraine headaches for ten years. I have been deserted by friends, lied to, stolen from, and talked about in false and ungodly ways, but God has been faithful and I am still here with a good report and I am using my experience to help others. I know many of you have the same type of testimony. For our own preservation we absolutely must remember, recount, and recall the mighty things that God has done for us and others.

A party often commemorates a special occasion or an important event like a birthday, an anniversary, a retirement, or a special achievement. Although these types of memorials are necessary and good, the best ones are when we remember God's intervention in the past saving us from destruction. It fills us with fresh faith and hope, and it encourages us—another way of saying it is that it gives us courage. No wonder that God says He is to be remembered from generation to generation.

God told the Israelites to remember that they were slaves in Egypt and to remember all the miracles He did there to convince Pharoah to let them go. He told them to not be afraid of their enemies but to remember what He did to Pharoah and to all of Egypt (see Deut. 7:18). He told them to remember all the ways He led them in the wilderness to humble and prove them, and to see if they would keep His commandments or not (see Deut. 8:2). They were to remember the difficulty along the way and the mighty acts of God in delivering them. When they were thirsty He brought water out of a rock, and when they were hungry He rained manna for food out of the sky each morning. Their shoes and clothing did not wear out for forty years. Talk about needing a new outfit—that must have been the ultimate!

Jesus told His disciples and all those who would ever believe in Him to receive Holy Communion as a way of remembering His death and resurrection. He said that the bread was His body broken and the wine was His blood. As He shared the bread and wine with His disciples at the last supper He said, "Do this often in remembrance of me." It was established as an outward sign of an inner faith and it is something very important that we should do also.

Don't take communion just once a month, or however often you do it, as a ritual, but take the time to remember what Jesus did on the cross. Don't just go out for dinner on your wedding anniversary, but take the time to talk about the years you and your spouse have had together. Talk about the hard times and the good times. When another year is gone and it is your birthday again, don't let it pass you by without remembering the things you have accomplished in life, the friends you have had, and the times you laughed so hard that your belly hurt. When I had my birthday dinner recently my son said, "Let's tell stories." I knew what he meant because we have done it before, and those times have turned out to be our best evenings together.

I asked him what he remembered most about growing up and he recalled several events. Some I had forgotten, some I had never known, and others I had heard before, but they were all touching and worth remembering. Dave and I shared things we remembered about him and somehow when the evening was over we felt closer. He even sent me a text message the next day saying what a blast he and his wife had with us the night before. Believe me, when you are in your sixties, and you have a child in his twenties who tells you that he had a blast with you—it is something to remember! Laugh a lot with your children. They want you to be fun to be with. Refrain from finding something wrong with the way they dress or style their hair, or what they choose to eat. When you get time with your grown children turn it into a party. You had the first part of their life to correct them, now it is God's turn. From now on you get to enjoy them.

There are 161 references to the word "remember" in the Bible concordance, sixty-two for the word "remembered" and four for "remembering." There are sixty-five references to the word "forget," and most of those are reminding us not to forget what God has done and how He has delivered us in the past.

There are times to forget and things to forget. For example, when the Apostle Paul said that he forgot what was behind, he was talking about not being condemned over past mistakes (see Phil. 3:13). In Isaiah we are taught not to earnestly remember the things of old because God is doing a new thing. All that means is that we are not to get stuck in the past and never want or be ready for change. We hear a lot of teaching about forgetting the past and although there are times to do that, we should also be taught to remember the past and pass it on to future generations.

History is His-Story

Any history book is simply an account of what has happened in the past. In America we now find that the history books have been revised and most of the references about God have been taken out of them. We no longer have our true history easily available, and that is a tragedy. History books in public schools are written without references to God or His word, so in reality what the students are taught is not true history at all. America was founded by godly men and women, on the word of God.

Our constitution and law books were based on the word of God. The government buildings in our capital have the word of God etched in the walls and foundation stones. America is great because she has been godly, but if the Humanists have their way and are successful in removing the memory of what God has done in America, then she will be destroyed or at the very least become a country we will not be proud to live in. (Our ministry does have American history books available that contain our country's true godly heritage.)

The devil is using ungodly people to keep Americans and the world from remembering what God has done in our past. The amazing growth, power, wealth, and creative genius we experienced in such a short period of time in the United States was nothing less than amazing, and it was all because of God. Man must not now try to push God out and take the credit themselves, because if they do, the result may be something we will truly not want to remember.

The Bible is a history book of God's story, and He warned that no one should add to it or take from it. A person deciding to change a history book does not alter the history but does keep people from knowing it. If we don't know where we came from we usually don't know what direction to take as we go forward. If our history was good we can repeat it and if it was bad then we can avoid repeating it. History, good or bad, is all educational. Most of us want to know what has happened in the past. We like to hear people's stories, which is their history. We like to go to museums and see movies about past wars and tragic events like the sinking of the *Titanic* or Hitler and the Holocaust. We are interested simply because it is history and as such it is part of us. We feel more complete when we know our history.

The Internet offers Web sites that help people establish their family trees and I have often wondered if I have any preachers or ministers in my family bloodline. Are there any men or women who did great things, any writers, or inventors? History beckons to us to dig in and find out what she holds.

Most of us are born curious. We like to search out a mystery and history is filled with mystery. I know I, for one, am amazed when I read about some of the battles that the Israelites fought, and the variety of ways that God delivered them. Knowing history increases our faith that if God did it once, He can do it again.

If we don't pass the true story of God down to the next generations it will be tragic. Only truth can keep people free. Tell your children everything you can about God. Tell them Bible stories and help them remember the great things that God has done. Be sure when you celebrate holidays like Christmas, Easter, and Thanksgiving that you use them as an opportunity to teach your children and to remind yourself of what they are truly about. Christmas is the day we celebrate the birth of Jesus Christ. We honor Him by giving gifts to one another. People historically give to the poor at Christmastime more than any other time of the year. Christmas is a Christian holiday, but many people celebrate it who have no specific religious affiliation. It is just a day that they get together with family, go to office parties, and give and receive gifts, but they have no understanding of what it is really all about. We don't want to let ourselves fall into the trap of observing traditions that have lost their meaning.

Thanksgiving is not just a day to eat turkey and pumpkin pie. It was a day originally set aside to remember and give thanks to God for what He had done in protecting the first men and women who came to America to flee religious persecution in Europe. It was a type of harvest celebration like the one that the Jews celebrated. A day to give thanks for the crops they were able to harvest. We should always take time at Thanksgiving to actually give thanks and it should be a prayer of more than thirty seconds. I suggest sitting in a group with family or friends and letting each person share something in particular they are thankful for that happened in the past year as well as sharing their gratitude in general.

Easter is a celebration of the resurrection of Jesus Christ and should not focus on hunting colored eggs and getting baskets filled with chocolate delivered by a rabbit. I am not against the Easter bunny or Easter egg hunts, but we definitely need to tell our children what the holiday truly represents. These special holidays and others were instituted as memorials, or ways to remember great things that God did in the past, so let us make sure that we remember. Before you sit down to a meal with family on Easter, why not get your Bible out and read the story of the resurrection and offer a special prayer of thanks for what God has done for us through Christ?

Remember That God Remembers

It increases our faith when we remember that God remembers us. He promises to never leave us or forsake us. He keeps one eye on us all the time. He remembers all of our prayers. He keeps our tears in a bottle, and does not forget the cry of the humble, poor, and afflicted (see Ps. 56:8 and 9:12).

Just yesterday I spoke with a man whose wife died of cancer at the age of thirty-nine, leaving him with four children and a broken heart. He shared how he just thought he could not go on until he read Psalm 121, reminding him that God is his Keeper.

> He will not allow your foot to slip or to be moved; He Who keeps you will not slumber.
>
> *Psalm 121:3*

> The Lord will keep your going out and your coming in from this time forth and forevermore.
>
> *Psalm 121:8*

This man needed to be reminded that even though he had experienced a tragedy, God had not forgotten him. God was watching over him and would enable him to do what needed to be done. God would strengthen him.

A short time later he met a wonderful woman who had also endured a tragedy in her marriage. They fell in love, married, and together they have raised their seven children. Tragedy is not the end of life, but it can be a new beginning. We may never understand why some things happen the way they happen, but no matter what happens, God is still God and He has not forgotten you.

God forgives and forgets our sins (see Heb. 10:17), but He never forgets us.

CHAPTER

8

Celebrate Who You Are and What You Have

Are you in the habit of looking at what you are not and what you don't have, or have you trained yourself to see who you are, what you can do, and the resources you currently have available? We need to learn to identify with Christ and acknowledge the good things that are in us.

> That the communication of thy faith may become effectual by the acknowledging of every good thing which is in you in Christ Jesus.
>
> *Philemon 1:6 KJV*

We easily form a habit of acknowledging the bad things we do, but according to this Scripture we need to acknowledge the good things in us through Christ Jesus in order for our faith to be effectual.

The Apostle Paul prayed that we would have a spirit of wisdom and revelation in the knowledge of God and the Lord Jesus

Christ, that the eyes of our heart would be flooded with light so we might know the hope of His calling and the riches of the glory of the inheritance that is ours. He also prayed that we would know the exceeding greatness of God's power toward us who believe in Him (see Eph. 1:17–19).

It is very important that we have a spirit of wisdom and revelation that we might know the following three things: Number one, that we might have the knowledge of God, or that we may know God Himself. This is not knowledge gained through education, but it is knowledge gained through revelation. It is a knowing that is revealed to us by God Himself. Number two is that we might know the hope of our calling, which means the eternal plan of God and how we fit into it. God wants a possession and we are that possession. We are His desired family. We must know that God is calling us to be His sons and daughters and that as such we have an inheritance. An inheritance becomes activated when the one giving the inheritance dies, and since Jesus has died we must realize that we have an inheritance now. We are not waiting for one, but we have one now! Number three is the revelation knowledge of God's power that is available to us. We can do anything that God asks us to do because of the greatness of His power toward us. Paul states that this power of which we are speaking cannot be measured; it is unlimited and surpasses even the greatest thing we can imagine. Have many of us have even begun to know this power? If this power is already available to us, then why do so many of God's children live broken-down lives, filled with depression, discouragement, and despair? We must not be afraid to ask these questions if we are to find answers.

Truly Know God

How wonderful it is that we may know the God of the Universe! The Athenians built an altar to the unknown God (see Acts 17:23). With all of their education, reasoning, and philosophies, they still could not understand God. The Bible teaches us that eternal life is to know God.

> And this is eternal life: [it means] to know (to perceive, recognize, become acquainted with, and understand) You, the only true and real God, and [likewise] to know Him, Jesus [as the] Christ (the Anointed One, the Messiah), Whom You have sent.
>
> *John 17:3*

When Paul prayed for the Ephesians, they knew God and had eternal life, but still Paul prayed for them to have wisdom and revelation concerning knowing Him. They still needed to know Him more. Knowing God is progressive and must be sought after. Paul shares his deepest desire with us in Philippians. Please take time to digest this Scripture:

> [For my determined purpose is] that I may know Him [that I may progressively become more deeply and intimately acquainted with Him, perceiving and recognizing and understanding the wonders of His Person more strongly and more clearly], and that I may in that same way come to know the power outflowing from His resurrection.
>
> *Philippians 3:10*

There is a big difference in knowing about God and knowing God. When we truly know God, we also experience (know) His power. Paul was determined and he understood that the knowing he sought would be a lifelong pursuit. He knew that the attaining of this knowledge was not something to be gotten by reasoning or from book learning, but it had to be given by revelation from God and would be acquired progressively throughout his life. Thankfully, God is deep enough that we will never know all there is to know. Only when we go to Heaven will we be known even as He knows us now (see 1 Cor. 13:12).

It saddens me when people frequently equate Christianity with going to church and nothing more. In church we are taught about God, but an intimate personal relationship with God through Jesus Christ requires much more than a weekly trip to church. To know Him we must be hungry for the type of knowledge that can only come from God Himself through revelation. It is a knowing that goes beyond what we think, see, or feel. It is an inner knowledge of God that cannot be taken from us through anything or anyone. When we have this inner knowledge, nothing outward can sway us from our belief in God. We no longer need evidence to protect our faith. We trust God just as much if He does not give us what we want as we would if He did. We do not need feeling or seeing, because we know. Job said, "I know that my Redeemer and Vindicator lives" (Job 19:25). Even though Job went through unimaginably difficult and seemingly unfair things, He knew God, and his knowledge carried him through the difficulties and brought him to a new level of victory and blessing.

Many Christians live too much by feeling. If they feel joyful and happy then they say God is blessing them, but if they feel blah, cold, or flat then they might be heard asking, "Where is God today?" If their prayer is not answered to their satisfaction they ask where God is. When we experienced the bombing of the Twin Towers in New York City on 9/11, a newscaster asked, "Where was God when all of this happened?" Had this newscaster known God, he would never have asked such a question.

If we have a true knowledge of God we are not disturbed by any scientific view, nor any theories of evolution, nor so-called contradictions in Bible translations. We have come to a perfect rest that God is, and knowing that, then we know that nothing else matters. We do not feel a need to explain things because we know what cannot be explained in words. Paul said that he saw things when he had visions of Heaven that he could not explain. Men always want to explain God, but if we know Him truly, then the first thing we give up is trying to understand Him or explain Him. The person who knows spiritually has no need to understand mentally.

Pray daily for a spirit of wisdom and revelation that you might know God and His Christ, the Messiah, the Anointed One. Celebrate that you know God, that you are an eternal being and that you are progressively coming to know Him better as each day passes by. What an amazing blessing it is to know God. It should make us sing, dance, clap our hands, and shout for joy. Celebrate because you have joined Jesus' party!

Know God's Call and Inheritance

God wants us to know what His eternal plan and purpose are. He wants us to know the hope of our calling. He has chosen us in Himself to be holy, to live before Him without blemish and in love. This is God's call and it is great indeed. How can we meet such a calling since we are filled with weakness, inability, and the liability to temptation? How can we be so flawed and yet have the hope of being holy? It is beautifully simple when we have revelation. We are made holy in Jesus Christ and we can lift up our voices and confess out loud, "I am holy in Jesus Christ, I am blameless and perfect in Him." When any believer comes to the place of knowing by revelation what is his *right now*, he puts an end to searching relentlessly for something, because he now knows that he has it! It is finished! It is done! It is his! He can then easily become what he believes that he is. What I just said in the last six sentences is extremely important for each person to grasp, so I ask you to reread it. We must understand what we have right now, otherwise we will spend our lives struggling to obtain something that has been ours all along.

I tried for many years to love other people, but I had no revelation that God loved me and that I was in fact filled with the love of God (see Rom. 5:5). It was easy for me to give love away once I knew that I had it, but as long as I was stuck trying to get something I already had, I was unable to give it. We cannot give away what we do not realize that we have! No wonder the Apostle Paul prayed for the church at Ephesus to know what they had inherited in Christ. Perhaps the reason we have difficulty accepting that holiness, peace, joy, righteousness, redemption, deliverance, wisdom, victory, and literally hundreds of others blessings are ours right now is because of the way we see ourselves. We often look at ourselves as mere human beings rather than as children of God. We need to see what God sees. We need to look with the eye of faith. We may think the things promised are ours after we change and behave better, so we keep trying to improve and tragically we never learn to come as we are.

You Are Invited to a "Come as You Are" Party

One of the first things we ask when we are invited to a party is, "How should I dress?" Most of us like it best when we feel that we can come as we are. We like it when we can relax and be ourselves. I noticed this Scripture not too long ago and thought about how marvelous it is and what a message of acceptance it brings:

> It is through Him that we have received grace (God's unmerited favor) and [our] apostleship to promote obedience to the faith and make disciples for His name's sake among all the nations.
>
> And this includes you, called of Jesus Christ and invited [as you are] to belong to Him.
>
> *Romans 1:5–6*

If you skipped over the Scripture please go back and read it and particularly notice that you are invited as you are. God will work in you by His Holy Spirit and help you become all that you need to be, but you can come as you are. You don't have to stand afar and only hear the music of the party, you are invited to attend.

You have joy and peace today. You are redeemed, accepted, and made right with God. You are! Not "you will be someday."

We are destined to be molded into His image and nothing can stop it if we will simply come when He invites us. We don't have to clean up our act first. We don't have to put on a religious demeanor and get out our religious tone of voice.

Our view of God, ourselves, and His plan for us is too small. God wants us to come out of smallness and see the greatness of His calling and our inheritance in Him. When we inherit a thing it means that we get what someone else worked for. Jesus gained a prize for us. He worked for what we inherit, and all we can do is receive it by faith. Nothing else is required. Dave and I will leave our children an inheritance. They know about it and will enjoy it when we die. At that time they will not need to do anything but receive it and enjoy what Dave and I worked our whole lives to be able to pass on to them. Can we by faith receive what God has already done for us on the cross? We should not be waiting for Him to do anything, because He has done all that needs to be done. We need revelation knowledge concerning what He has done that it is ours right now. One step of faith will put you in the middle of the greatest inheritance ever passed from one person to another. That step of faith takes the struggle and frustration out of life. As 1 John 4:17 says, even "as He is, so are we in this world." That is good news!

We Need Vision

We do not need more of anything, but we do need vision concerning what we already have. We need vision to do greater things for the glory of God. When we truly know God and we see the hope of His calling and our inheritance, we will step up to do greater things. Smallness will no longer satisfy us because we know that we have a great God and a great calling.

When God revealed Himself to Isaiah, the first thing Isaiah did was to recognize the importance and power of words and how vain many of his had been in the past (see Isa. 6:1–5). He saw the holiness of God, and he had a revelation of God that brought him to a place of repentance over some things concerning his words. Perhaps it was his small talk about God that convicted him.

Jesus asked Peter who people said that the Son of Man was, and Peter replied, "Some say John the Baptist; others say Elijah; and others Jeremiah or one of the prophets." Then Jesus asked Peter, "Who do you say that I am?" God is listening to what we say about Him, about ourselves, and the plan of God for our lives. He listens to see if we know Him and our inheritance in Him. Peter said, "You are the Christ, the Son of the living God" (Matt. 16:13–16). Jesus went on to tell Peter that his knowledge had been revealed to him by God.

The other people looked at Jesus naturally and reasoned as to who He might be. As we can see by their answers, they really had no accurate knowledge. But Peter had revelation and Jesus told him that on that revelation God would build His church and the gates of hell would not prevail against it.

I tell you truly that when we know God, know His call and inheritance, and go on to know His power, then the gates of hell cannot ever prevail against us. We will do great things and have joyful lives regardless of our circumstances. We will live in the spirit of celebration because of what we know in our hearts.

Let Me Tell You What I Know

"Let me tell you what I know" would normally be a statement filled with pride, but in this case I have a purpose. I want to tell you what I know about you and me as Christians, and I am going to do it from memory without looking anything up in the Bible.

I know that we *are* children of God, and that we *are* called, anointed, and appointed by Him for greatness. We *are* destined to bring God glory and be molded into the image of Jesus Christ. We *have* (not will have) righteousness, peace, and joy in the Holy Spirit. We *are* forgiven for all of our sins and our names *are* written in the Lamb's Book of Life. Jesus *has* gone before us to prepare a place for us that where He is we may be also.

I know that until He returns for us, He *has* sent His Holy Spirit as our guarantee of the even greater good things that *are* to come. We *are* guaranteed an inheritance for it *was* purchased with the blood of Jesus. We have a new covenant and are offered a new way of living. We *are* made new creatures in Christ, old things *have* passed away and all things *have* become brand new. We can let go of past mistakes, and press toward the mark of perfection. I know that *God loves us* with an everlasting, unconditional love and that His mercy endures forever. I know that all things *are* possible with God and *we can* do all things through Christ Who is our Strength.

I know that God never allows more to come on us than we can bear, but He always provides a way out, a safe place to land. I know that *all* things work together for good to those who love God and *are* called according to His purpose and that what our enemies mean for harm, God intends for good. I know that *He is* our Vindicator, our Redeemer, and Restorer. He makes all things new.

> I know that God never allows more to come on us than we can bear, but He always provides a way out, a safe place to land.

We don't have to worry because God has all power in Heaven and on the earth and even under the earth, and He has everything under control. I know that God hears and answers our prayers. I know that God is our Keeper and we *are* safe. We *have been* set free from the power of sin, we *are* seated in heavenly places with Christ Jesus and we *are* made acceptable to God through faith in Jesus.

The truth is that I could go for a while longer, but I think by now you have the point. Before I knew these things I had no power, no victory, and no hope, but now I know that my Redeemer lives! I know that we should be celebrating what we have right now, for truly we have more than enough in every area of life! All of these wonderful things are currently ours through our faith in Jesus Christ. In Him we are new creatures; old things have passed away and all things are made new (see 2 Cor. 5:17). I quoted Philemon 1:6 from the King James Version of the Bible in the previous chapter, but take a look at it in the Amplified Translation:

[And I pray] that the participation in and sharing of your faith may produce and promote full recognition and

appreciation and understanding and precise knowledge of
every good [thing] that is ours in [our identification with]
Christ Jesus [and unto His glory].

Philemon 1:6

Paul prayed that the Christians would know the good things
that were currently theirs, and that is my prayer for you.

Paul prayed that the Christians would know the good things
that were currently theirs, and that is my prayer for you.

Know the Power of God

In the letter to the Ephesians, Paul prayed that we would know
the exceeding greatness of God's power toward us. God is powerful and anyone who believes in God surely believes that, but
the question is—do we believe that His power is available to us
and that it exists for us? Paul spoke of God's power toward us!

I lived in total defeat the first forty or so years of my life
because I did not know that I had power as a Christian. I
thought I just had to put up with whatever came my way and
try to muddle through until I died, at which time I could go to
Heaven. I can tell you for sure that a life as I have just described
does not give glory to God as we are called to do. We must know
His power toward us!

This is a power that has already been given. In Luke, Jesus
said, "Behold I have given you power...". We do not need to
strive for power or hope to have power someday—we have

power now! The same power that raised Christ from the dead dwells in us (see Rom. 8:11) and we can be quickened (filled with life) by that power. This is not a onetime filling that then slowly drains away as the days go by, but we can be daily filled and even moment by moment we can experience His presence and power in our lives. The starting place is to believe! We must believe what God tells us in His word and we must believe it beyond doubt. Even if we don't feel powerful we must believe that we have power, and it is not an effort to do so if we have revelation knowledge concerning God's power toward us.

God's power is indeed great and it is so great that unless God opens our spiritual eyes (gives us revelation) we will never grasp it. We have no way to determine how great God's power is because it cannot be measured and it has no limits. The good news is that it is toward us. This good news is so exciting that I think I feel a party coming on! I think I need to eat a cookie or buy a pair of shoes or do something that makes me laugh; I need to celebrate because I know that I will never be left in a position of being without power!

This is better than knowing the head of the local power company. I have to pay for the power that comes into my home, but the power that I live by has been paid for by Jesus Christ. If the power company called and told us that we had been selected to have free power the rest of our lives, we would get so excited that before long everyone we know would know about the power available to us. We would not have to worry about turning off lights, or how much our hot water heater ran. And, what if the power company guaranteed us power even during a storm? We would not need to fear storms. We could look up and down the dark streets all around us during a storm, but our lights and power would still be on. That is the way it works when you are hooked into God's unlimited power by faith.

We are living in hard and perilous times, but the darkness cannot put out our light because we have free, unlimited power. I am excited and I feel like celebrating, so I think I will take a break from my work, go make myself a wonderful latte, hug my dog, and give my husband a big kiss!

CHAPTER
9

Celebrate You

I am back! The latte was great and so was the kiss.

Now we need to talk about celebrating you, because you are valuable, and definitely someone worth a celebration! I cannot write a book without telling you how awesome you are and what great possibilities you have. I am afraid that perhaps nobody else has ever told you, and I just cannot let you go one more day without knowing the truth. You are fearfully and wonderfully made and you are made for a purpose. As a believer in Jesus Christ you are the home of God—yes, God lives inside of you (see Eph. 3:17).

> Now we need to talk about celebrating you, because you are valuable, and definitely someone worth a celebration!

He has invested Himself in you and given you talents and abilities that equip you to do certain things. You are part of God's plan and purpose.

What Do You Think of Yourself?

Have you ever taken time to think about what you think about yourself? God thinks that you are special and He celebrates you all the time. What is your attitude toward you? Are you worth a celebration? In the Bible we are told to sing, shout, rejoice, and be in high spirits because God has taken away the judgment that was against us. He has come to live in the midst of us and we have no need to fear. Because He loves us He does not even mention past sins, and He exults over us with singing (see Zeph. 3:14, 17).

> God thinks that you are special and He celebrates you all the time.

These Scriptures don't say that God is sitting in Heaven crying and mourning because we make mistakes and are not all that He had hoped we would be. They say that we should be in high spirits (a good mood) because God loves us and is singing over us. It sounds like a party to me!

When one lost sheep is found the shepherd rejoices (see Matt. 18:13), so if you just became a believer in Jesus yesterday, God is rejoicing over you. You may have a long way to go before reaching spiritual maturity, and you may have many faults that need to be dealt with, but God is still rejoicing over you. He is always happy about how far we have come no matter how far we still have to go. God always celebrates progress!

God Is Smiling over You

God is pleased with you! Now, before you decide to reject that piece of good news let me give you some scriptural backing for my statement. On two different occasions, a voice (God's voice) came out of Heaven saying that He was pleased with His Son Jesus (see Luke 3:22 and Matt. 17:5). The first time this occurred was at Jesus' baptism and the second time was when He and a few of His disciples were on the Mount of Transfiguration. Both of these events were major ones in the life of Jesus and I am sure that what God said was intended to add to the celebration and encourage Jesus.

You are probably thinking as I did upon initially seeing these Scriptures, "I can understand God saying that to Jesus because He was perfect." The Holy Spirit was trying to use these Scriptures to encourage me to stop thinking that God was mad at me most of the time and to dare to believe that He was actually pleased with me. Like many Christians who lack revelation I had the mistaken idea that every time I did something wrong God was frowning and was a little bit angry at me. That had been my experience with my earthly father and I assumed God was the same way, but I was wrong. The Psalmist David, the little shepherd boy who became king, believed that God was pleased with him and yet we know from Scripture that David was far from perfect.

He brought me forth also into a large place; He was delivering me because He was pleased with me and delighted in me.

Psalm 18:19

This statement also came out of David's mouth as part of a song that he sang to God on the day the Lord delivered him from all of his enemies and the hand of Saul (see 2 Sam. 22:1, 20). Just imagine walking around the house or driving in your car singing, "God is pleased with me and He delights in me!" I doubt that many of us would have that kind of confidence, but we should. David also said that he knew God favored him and was delighted in him because his enemies did not triumph over him (see Ps. 41:11).

Perhaps David was a little overly zealous and had an attitude problem. After all, who would have the audacity to say that God was pleased with him? But, we must also remember that God said David was a man after His own heart, so that means He liked his bold attitude of faith. It may have been one of the main reasons that God chose and anointed him to be king. David wasn't the only one who talked like this. The Apostle John also spoke of himself as being the disciple whom Jesus loved (esteemed and was delighted in) (see John 13:23).

After much study, I finally had to agree with the Holy Spirit. God is not mad at us, and He is actually pleased with us and delights in us. I believe that God is smiling over us right now! He sees us in and through Jesus Christ. Are you ready to acknowledge who you are in Christ and every good thing that is yours in Him (see Phil. 1:6)?

> I believe that God is smiling over us right now!

God gave Moses words to bless the Israelites with:

The Lord bless you and watch, guard, and keep you;

The Lord make His face to shine upon and enlighten you and be gracious (kind, merciful, and giving favor) to you;

The Lord lift up His [approving] countenance upon you and give you peace (tranquility of heart and life continually).

Numbers 6:24–26

Don't fail to notice the phrase "approving countenance." God is smiling over you!

I once had a pastor who spoke these words over the congregation at the close of each church service. What would happen to us if we actually believed that God is smiling at us, that He approves of us? I believe it would add a high degree of confidence and boldness that is actually necessary not only for the enjoyment of life, but also in order to accomplish the will of God. If you have the courage to begin speaking over yourself that God is pleased and delighted in you, I can promise you that the first few times you will feel embarrassed. You might even blush, but you will also begin to walk with new levels of confidence, power, peace, and joy.

As I say often—God is not pleased with all of our behavior, but He is pleased with us if we love Him and want to make progress. When we make positive confessions, such as I am suggesting, we are not talking about our behavior, but we are talking about our heart.

Is It Dangerous to Have a Good Opinion of Yourself?

Pride is a terrible sin, and we are instructed in God's word not to think more highly of ourselves than we ought to. We are told not to have an exaggerated opinion of ourselves (see Rom. 12:3). That doesn't mean that we need to have a bad opinion of or look down on ourselves. It does mean that we are to remember that we are no better than anyone else and that whatever God has enabled us to do is a gift from Him. It is never a reason to have an exalted opinion of ourselves. We have no more right to claim credit for a special ability we have than we do for blue eyes or brown hair. Paul wrote to the Corinthians and asked them what they had that did not come as a gift from God (see 1 Cor. 4:7).

When we are warned not to think more highly of ourselves than we ought to, it means that we are to realize that we are nothing apart from Jesus and without Him we can do nothing. The value we have is found in Him and we can celebrate who we are only because of Him. Actually, when we celebrate who we are in Jesus, it is a way of celebrating Jesus Himself.

We make this a lot more difficult than it needs to be. It is simple—we are everything in Jesus and nothing in ourselves. I like to say, "I am an everything/nothing!" We celebrate because of the amazing work God does in us, and not because of any worth we have in ourselves. As long as we continue giving God the glory for anything good that we manifest we are on a safe and right track.

For some reason religion has taught people that to be godly

they must have a low, or even bad, opinion of themselves, and I believe this kind of thinking has done incalculable damage to the plan of God. I think that as long as we know we are lower

> For some reason religion has taught people that to be godly they must have a low, or even bad, opinion of themselves, and I believe this kind of thinking has done incalculable damage to the plan of God.

than God and He is always our Chief and Head then we are safe. Consider these Scriptures:

> What is man that You are mindful of him, and the son of [earthborn] man that You care for him?
>
> Yet you have made him but a little lower than God [or heavenly beings], and You have crowned him with glory and honor.
>
> You made him to have dominion over the works of Your hands; You have put all things under his feet.
>
> *Psalm 8:4–6*

Yes, we are lower than God, but He has crowned us with honor and glory. Do you have an honoring attitude toward yourself or a disrespectful one? We are made in the image of God (see Gen. 1:26) and He has given us authority over all the other works of His hands. God wants to work in partnership with us to accomplish His purpose on the earth, and we cannot do that unless we maintain a proper attitude toward ourselves.

I suggest that you say out loud daily, "I am nothing without Jesus, but in and through Him I am valuable and I can do great things."

> Do you have an honoring attitude toward yourself or a disrespectful one?

I don't think it's dangerous to have a good opinion of yourself (in Christ), but I do think *it is dangerous not to.* The truth is that you cannot rise above what you think. We are all limited by our own thinking. If we think small, we will live small. And if we think big, we will live big. God wants us to realize how big He is and He wants us to be bold enough to think big thoughts. God did not chastise David because he thought he could kill Goliath—He was proud of him! David knew that his victory was in God and not in himself, but he was confident and courageous and refused to live small.

What your life amounts to is directly connected to what you think of yourself. We need to learn to think like God thinks. We must learn to identify with Christ and the new person He has made us to be. Some identify with the problems they have had in life and call themselves by that name. They say, "I am divorced. I am bankrupt. I am an abuse victim. I am an alcoholic." They should say, "I was divorced, but now I am a new creature in Christ. I was a victim of abuse, but now I have a new

> What your life amounts to is directly connected to what you think of yourself. We need to learn to think like God thinks.

life and a new identity. I was an alcoholic, but now I am free and I have discipline and self-control." He has a good plan for each of us, but we must have our minds renewed (learn to think differently) if we ever hope to experience what Jesus purchased with His death and resurrection.

In Scripture God uses words like "beautiful," "honored," "valued," and "precious" when He is speaking of His people. There is no doubt that we are way less than perfect, that we have faults and weaknesses. We make mistakes and bad choices, and often lack wisdom, but God is God and He views us the way He knows we can be. He sees us as a finished project while we are making the journey. He sees the end from the beginning and is not worried about what takes place in between. He is not pleased with our sin and bad behavior, but He will never give up on us and He always encourages us to press on. God believes in you!

Does This Kind of Talk Frighten You?

When I initially began to see these kinds of things in Scripture I was afraid to even think this way, let alone really believe it. I was accustomed to thinking I was a terrible wreck of a person, a lowly worm and undeserving of anything except punishment. My whole identity was based on what I did, and since that wasn't very impressive it left me with a poor opinion of myself.

I was afraid that I would offend God if I dared to have a good thought about myself. I equated good thoughts about myself with pride. I had heard plenty of sermons concerning the danger of pride and was trying to be what I thought was humble.

I felt safe as long as I dared not think a good thought about myself. As I said earlier in the book, "I did not feel right if I did not feel wrong."

I should also mention that the negative attitude I had about myself was not something I was even consciously aware of. It was just the way I lived because I did not know any better. I can explain it now as being self-defeating, ungodly, wrong, and tragic, but that is a result of the knowledge I now possess of God's word. I often ask people if they have ever given any thought to what they think about themselves. Most people have never thought about it at all and seem reluctant to do so. Someone could be filled with self-depreciation, self-hatred, self-pity, or even pride and arrogance and not know it. We just don't think about what we think about ourselves, but we need to. I strongly suggest that you have a meeting with yourself and ask yourself some pointed questions regarding how you feel and think about yourself. You cannot deal with a problem if you don't know it even exists.

The devil hates books like this because they bring hidden things into the light. Satan works in darkness, but when light comes in and his works and lies are exposed he is easily defeated. It is time for you to celebrate you! It is time for you to celebrate your progress, your strengths and abilities. It is time for you to celebrate God in your life.

Learn to Live on the Resurrection Side of the Cross

We must live on the resurrection side of the cross. Jesus was crucified and raised from the dead so that we might no longer be stuck in sin, living lowly, wretched, miserable lives. Many people wear a necklace called a crucifix, which is an emblem of Jesus hanging on the cross. Often we see a crucifix in a church with Jesus hanging on it. I know it is done to remember and honor Him and I am not against it, but the truth is that He is not on the cross any longer. He is seated in heavenly places with His Father and has also lifted us above the low level of thinking and living of most of the world.

The Apostle Paul said that he was determined to know Jesus and the power of His resurrection that would lift Him out from among the dead (see Phil. 3:10). Jesus came to lift us out of the ordinary, out of negative thinking, guilt, shame, and condemnation. He came to take our sin to the cross and defeat it. It has no power over us any longer because we are forgiven and the penalty has been paid.

Which side of the cross are you living on: the crucifixion side or the resurrection side? It is good and respectful to remember that Jesus suffered a terrible death for us on the cross, but we need to also realize that He rose from the dead and made a new life available to us. There is a popular song entitled "Because He Lives," and it is about that fact that Jesus' death and resurrection give us the power and privilege to live life today in victory. Because He lives we can love ourselves in an unselfish way. A way that enables us to be all we can be for God's glory. The only way I know to say it is: get a new attitude about yourself! Stop thinking that your failures and mistakes are too much for God. He has cast all of your sins behind His back (see Isa. 38:17). He isn't looking at them and you need to stop looking at them, too. Deal with them in Christ and go on!

Celebrate Your Life

How do you feel about your life? Do you like it, love it, and enjoy it, or do you hate it and wish you had a different one than you have? Do you look at other people and their lives and wish you were them and had their lives? Do you want to look the way they look, own what they own, have their career or their family?

Wanting what others have is called coveting in the Bible and it is forbidden by God. He even included it in the Ten Commandments:

> You shall not covet your neighbor's house, your neighbor's wife, or his manservant, or his maidservant, or his ox, or his donkey, or anything that is your neighbor's.
>
> *Exodus 20:17*

You are never going to have anyone else's life, so wanting it is a waste of time. You won't look like them either, so learn to do the best you can with what you have to work with.

I have adopted a new phrase lately and it is helping me to deal with reality and not waste my time being upset about things I cannot do anything about. I have been saying, "It is what it is!" Somehow, that is a reality check for me and I quickly realize I need to deal with things the way they are, not the way I wish they were.

Nobody has a perfect life, and it is entirely possible that if you want someone else's life, they are busy wanting someone else's too; perhaps they even want your life. Unknown people want to be movie stars and movie stars want privacy. The regular employee wants to be the boss and the boss wishes he did not have so much responsibility. A single woman wants to be married and quite often a married woman wishes she were single. Contentment with life is not a feeling, but it is a decision we must make. Contentment does not mean that we never want to see change or improvement, but it does mean that we will do the best we can with what we have. It also means that we will maintain an attitude that allows us to enjoy the gift of life.

> Nobody has a perfect life, and it is entirely possible that if you want someone else's life, they are busy wanting someone else's too; perhaps they even want your life.

If we were to walk into the cancer ward of a hospital and ask a terminally ill patient if they would take our flawed life, they would probably be glad to do so. They probably would not think that our problems were anything to be upset about. If we put things in proper perspective they always look better. Today my back hurts a little because I have been sitting in the same position for days working on this book, but the good news is that I can walk and I even have access to Tylenol. I have been to places in India and Africa where something as simple as aspirin or Tylenol would be an amazing blessing.

The Nevertheless Principle

I once read a book that was based entirely on the word "nevertheless." It taught the reader to take every problem in their life, look at it honestly, and then say, "nevertheless," and find some offsetting positive thing in their life that brought the problem into perspective. It might sound something like this: "I have a lot of hard work to get accomplished in the next two weeks, nevertheless, after that my schedule is much more open, and I will be able to have some fun and get some extra rest." A mother may be weary and say, "My son who has Attention Deficit Disorder is driving me crazy, nevertheless, I do have a son, and I know many people who cannot have children at all." A father who has to work two jobs to make ends meet might say, "I am so tired of working all the time, nevertheless, I am thankful that God has provided me with jobs."

No matter who we are or what our challenge in life is, there is always a nevertheless. Some positive thing we can look at or talk about that brings the rest of life into perspective. Why don't you try it? The next time you are tempted to complain about your life in any way, go ahead and state your complaint, and then say, "nevertheless," and find something positive about your life to offset the complaint.

Just a Few Thoughts

If you woke up this morning with more body parts that don't hurt than those that do, you are blessed.

If you have food, clothes, and a place to live, you are richer than 75 percent of the world.

If you have money in the bank, in your wallet, or spare change at home, you are among the top 8 percent of the world's wealthiest people.

If you have never experienced the danger of battle, the lone-liness of imprisonment, the agony of torture, or the pangs of starvation, you are ahead of five hundred million people in the world.

If you can read this message, you are more blessed than two billion people in the world who cannot read.

Words Affect Moods

Something I have done to help me maintain a good attitude about my life is to say out loud, "I love my life." Our own words have an effect on our moods, so it is best to say something that will help you feel good rather than something that will make you mad or sad. Your life is what it is and, as they say, your atti-tude toward it can make or break you.

You can let staying happy be a fun challenge. See how many days you can go without getting into a bad mood or finding something in your life to complain about. Celebrating life is something we should do on purpose because we understand what a gift it is. God is life (see John 1:4), so in reality when we celebrate life we are celebrating God! Without Him there would be no life at all! Go ahead and try to create a better mood by saying, "I love my life." If you really want to feel good try this, "I love God, I love my life, I love myself, and I love people."

> See how many days you can go without getting into a bad mood or finding something in your life to complain about.

CHAPTER
10

Learn When to Stop

I share in my teaching that we often study the steps of Jesus, but fail to study the stops of Jesus. We all need to learn when to stop. Jesus stopped what He was doing to listen to people and to help them. He stopped to rest, to have dinner with friends, to make wine for a wedding, and to do lots of other simple but important things. One of my biggest problems for many years was that I simply did not know when to stop.

My chiropractor has told me to stop every forty-five minutes when I am writing, to get up and stretch out the muscles in my back so I don't end up in pain. But when I am in a flow, it is so hard to stop! If we don't know when to stop, we always end up with regrets later. Last night I lay in bed with my feet and legs aching because of my back, and it could have been avoided had I stopped occasionally to do what my doctor told me to do. Not knowing when to stop can cause all kinds of pain in our life.

When Jesus visited Mary and Martha, Mary knew when to stop, but Martha didn't. Mary sat at Jesus' feet so she could not miss the moment, but Martha just kept working (see Luke

10:38–41). I wonder how many times in my life I missed the moment because I would not stop working. I know I missed moments with my children when they were small because I valued work over playing with them. A good life is all about balance. We have to know when to start and when to stop many things. Ecclesiastes tells us there is a time for everything and that everything is beautiful in its time. Work is beautiful, but if we work when it is time to play then work is no longer beautiful. It can create a stress that has the ability to destroy our health. Play is beautiful, but if we play when we should be working, then play becomes a lack of discipline that can destroy us.

Stop to Laugh

It is important that we stop to laugh! The world is filled with reports of theft, violence, dishonesty, and corruption. If we don't laugh I don't how we will survive. The world does not always give us something to laugh about, so we need to create our own humor. Yesterday, Dave and I were driving in the car when he saw a sign advertising a certain item, and he said, "I bet that would cost an arm and a leg." I decided to be funny and said, "If you paid an arm and a leg for it you would have a hard time getting out of the store." He looked at me in disbelief and said, "You must be pretty desperate for a laugh." However, we both did laugh for quite a while, especially me. My joke was so unfunny that it was funny. Today we were both working out in the exercise room when he suddenly looked at me and said, "I can lift my leg above my head." I quickly saw a picture of him trying such a feat and thought, "If you lift your leg above your head you will fall over backward." He pressed the point that he could do it and said "Watch me!" He then lay down flat on his back and lifted his leg above his head and we both began to laugh. It was out of character for Dave and rather silly, but nonetheless it gave us both a good laugh.

I have found that life itself can be funnier than a supposedly funny movie. Out of desperation to laugh, I have watched comedians and funny movies, only to find that they are not always funny and I end up disappointed that I wasted my time. However, if we look at life in a more lighthearted way it can be very funny. We need to lighten up! My daughters often call me to share funny things the kids did or things they are noticing about the children's personalities as they are growing up. I am glad they take the time to share those things with me. We laugh, and then I tell Dave and he laughs, too. We could have missed the laughter if they would have been too busy to call or felt that it was unimportant. My daughter-in-law often sends me pictures of the baby doing cute and funny things. He might have a funny hat on, or some silly look on his face, but those pictures are a laugh break for me.

> We need to lighten up!

I am sure that several funny things happen to you every day if you will learn to look for them and realize how important it is to stop for laughter.

Let's stop to laugh:

Ever mindful of the congregation, the Baptist preacher and his wife decided to get a new dog, and they knew that the dog also had to be Baptist. They visited kennel after kennel and explained their needs. Finally, they found a kennel whose owner assured them he had just the dog they wanted. The owner brought the dog to meet the pastor and his wife.

"Fetch the Bible," he commanded. The dog bounded to the bookshelf, scrutinized the books, located the Bible, and brought it to the owner.

"Now find Psalm 23," he commanded. The dog dropped the Bible to the floor, and showing marvelous dexterity with his paws, leafed through, found the correct passage, and pointed to it with his paw.

The pastor and his wife were very impressed and purchased the dog. That evening, a group of church members came to visit. The pastor and his wife began to show off the dog, having him locate several Bible verses. The visitors were very impressed.

One man asked, "Can he do regular dog tricks, too?"

"I haven't tried yet," the pastor replied. He pointed his finger at the dog. "HEEL!" the pastor commanded. The dog immediately jumped on a chair, placed one paw on the pastor's forehead, and began to howl.

The pastor looked at his wife in shock and said, "Good Lord! He's Pentecostal!"

*   *   *

There was an airplane flying with four passengers. The pilot came back and said they were going to crash, but they only had three parachutes. He told them to decide among themselves who was going to get them. One was a Boy Scout, one was the smartest man in the world, one was an elderly man, and the last was a preacher. So, the preacher told them, "You take the parachutes because I know where I am going when I die and I am ready to go." The intellectual said, "Well, I have to have a parachute because I am the smartest man in the world." The elderly man told the preacher and the Boy Scout to take the two remaining parachutes because he had lived his life and was ready to go. The Boy Scout said, "There won't be a problem because the smartest man in the world just jumped out of the airplane with my backpack on."

*   *   *

The husband had just finished reading the book *Man of the House*. He stormed into the kitchen and walked directly up to his wife. Pointing a finger in her face, he said, "From now on, I want you to know that I am the man of this house, and my word is law! I want you to prepare me a gourmet meal tonight, and when I'm finished eating my meal, I expect a scrumptious dessert afterward. Then, after dinner, you're going to draw me my bath so I can relax. And when I'm finished with my bath, guess who's going to dress me and comb my hair?"

His wife replied, "THE FUNERAL DIRECTOR!"

*   *   *

A child came home from Sunday School and told his mother that he had learned a new song about a cross-eyed bear named Gladly. It took his mother a while before she realized that the hymn was really "Gladly the Cross I'd Bear."

*   *   *

I am desperate to laugh. I wasted too much of my life being mad and sad, and I have a lot of catching up to do. I am committed to taking every opportunity I can find to laugh; when I can't find one, I am going to try to make one. I think Jesus was playful and funny. I can imagine Him teasing His disciples and playing pranks on them. Maybe you don't see Jesus this way, but you cannot prove He wasn't this way so don't try to rain on my parade. I know that He was serious and sober minded, but He was always in perfect balance so He had to have humor, too.

If we look at the twelve men Jesus chose for disciples, it's clear that He had to have a sense of humor. They were emotional and competitive. They frequently doubted and were filled with reasoning that was often humorous in itself. Peter said some fairly ridiculous things to Jesus during their journey together, but Jesus chose him, and the rest of His disciples. His choices were not mistakes; they were chosen on purpose. Surely, Jesus wanted us to see from the choices He made that He takes us as we are and is not at all bothered by our faults. They did have many flaws; *nevertheless*, when Jesus called, they followed.

I am sure the three years they trained with Jesus were intense, but they were balanced with humor and rest.

Try to Keep Up with Children

Research shows that adults laugh approximately twenty-five times a day. Actually, I think twenty-five sounds high for most of the adults I know and am around. It is 3:00 PM where I am at right now, and I think I may have laughed five times so far today—but I promise to try to meet my quota before bedtime.

Jesus told us to become like little children. They can have fun in just about any kind of situation and they never fail to stop and laugh. According to statistics they laugh on average of four hundred times a day! I just spent five days with my one-year-old grandson, Travis, and I laughed more in those five days than I normally do in two months. He has learned to laugh out loud and so he does it for no reason at all. He just suddenly laughs out loud and then, when we laugh at him laughing, he laughs again and again. He does it as long as we will keep the game going. He discovered how to open my glasses case and starting putting his baby spoon in it. Each time he got it open he laughed. When we clap for his progress, he claps for himself and laughs again. I can assure you that he is not worried, anxious, or thinking about all of his mistakes in life. No wonder Jesus told us to become like little children if we wanted to enter and enjoy His kingdom.

> Jesus told us to become like little children.

Stop to Rest

Resting is very important and most of us need to do it a lot more often than we do. Whatever happened to recess? When we were children in school we had morning recess, lunch, and afternoon recess. These were all times to eat and/or play and they were within a six- or seven-hour period of time. Suddenly when high school started, recess disappeared! Did we stop needing it because we became teenagers? The older we get, it seems, the less recess we get. But perhaps it should be the other way around. I have worked really hard since I was about thirteen years old and I am becoming fonder of recess every day. Recess is simply a break in normal business that allows us time to rest and relax.

I am going to take a short recess and I will be right back!

Ten minutes later: I am back and I feel much better!

Before I took my ten-minute break, I had to go to the bathroom, was thirsty, hungry, and stiff. I solved all of those issues in ten minutes and now I feel refreshed. When you start feeling exhausted, when you hear yourself sighing frequently, when your muscles are tense, and when your creativity has been reduced to zero, it is time to stop! We usually feel that we must press on because the job has to be finished, but the truth is that a short break makes us better in every way. It also enables us to enjoy what we are doing instead of resenting it. We must learn to control our workload and never let it control us.

Take a break when you need one, because you are worth it. Give yourself permission to rest! You are a human being, not a human doing. I promise that it is OK to rest! We all have limits and it is foolish not to admit them. Some days my tank is not as full as other days and I have stopped trying to figure out why. I just stop before I am totally running on empty and sucking dirt into my carburetor. My dad was an automobile mechanic and he always said, "Never let your gas tank get empty because you will suck dirt into your carburetor." If he found my gas tank close to empty he got upset, so I was careful to keep my tank at least half full. I wish I would have followed that advice with my life energy. If I had, I might have avoided some illness and laughed a lot more, and I am sure I would have accomplished just as much but enjoyed it more.

Most mistakes we make in life we cannot go back and undo, but we can learn from them and hopefully prevent someone else from making the same mistakes we did. So my advice to you from experience is: add more recesses into your life.

Take More Vacations

If I say, "Take more vacations," you might think that you would if you had more time off work or more money. But the truth is we can take vacations without money and we can take the time we do have and use it more wisely.

Try taking half days off, but don't use them to run errands, unless, of course, they are fun ones. If you can take vacation in one-hour increments, try taking two hours off to go to lunch with a good friend or relative you enjoy. When you do take time off, refer to it as vacation, not time off. The word "vacation" has a nice feeling and a good emotional effect.

I think we actually hesitate to say that we are on vacation too often because we don't want people to think we don't work hard enough. When someone finds out that I am taking some time off they usually say, "Oh, are you going on vacation?" and I often feel that I need to justify it by saying, "Yes, but I will be doing some work, too." I think I justified my existence on earth by working for so long that I still need to read my own books and take my own advice when it comes to the subject of vacation.

I recently spent some time with a friend who is an attorney

and as I shared with him the things in this book, he told me that he had taken three days of vacation and also felt the need to justify taking time off. A co-worker had called him and asked what he was doing while he was off work. He responded that he was going to play some golf, but that he would be doing business by phone and e-mail. We should be able to take time off without working and not feel guilty. We don't have to always be working in some way to justify our existence on earth.

Whenever possible, it's a good idea to take one or two vacations each year consisting of a week or more because it usually takes us a couple of days to actually gear down and unwind enough to reach the level of real rest. In the meantime, take the day, half-day, two-hour, and ten-minute vacations that are important to make life more balanced. Use holidays to rest and do things that will refresh you, and be sure to be with people who will make you laugh. The next chapter of this book is dedicated to giving your soul a vacation, so get ready for more celebration!

> Take the day, half-day, two-hour, and ten-minute vacations that are important to make life more balanced.

CHAPTER
11

Give Your Soul a Vacation

The subject of vacation is an important one, but our physical body is not the only part of us that needs vacation. Our souls need a vacation, too. Have you ever given your soul a vacation?

Your soul is comprised of your mind, will, and emotions, and it is a very important part of your entire being. You are a spiritual being and you live in a physical body. But if you don't understand your soul and the needs that it has, you will not be a whole, healthy individual.

You can take a vacation, thinking that you need a physical rest, but if you don't let your soul rest at the same time, you will return home just as exhausted as you were when you left. We can lie on the beach and worry, but that does not equal a vacation. We can take a day off and spend it emotionally upset trying to deal with personal problems, traffic, high prices, and

> We can lie on the beach and worry, but that does not equal a vacation.

rude people, and we would have been better off staying at work.

It is vitally important that we learn how to let our souls rest. Jesus said that if we are overburdened, weary, and worn out that we should come to Him and learn how He handled life. He said that He would give us rest for our souls. In the Amplified Translation of the Bible it says the type of rest He is talking about is recreation, refreshment, and blessed quiet for our souls. I pondered His statement and realized that Jesus was offering us a vacation for our souls (our inner lives). He offers us rest for our mind, wills, and emotions if we will come to Him and learn how He handles life.

> Come to Me, all you who labor and are heavy-laden and overburdened, and I will cause you to rest. [I will ease and relieve and refresh your souls.]
>
> Take My yoke upon you and learn of Me, for I am gentle (meek) and humble (lowly) in heart, and you will find rest (relief and ease and refreshment and recreation and blessed quiet) for your souls,
>
> For My yoke is wholesome (useful, good—not harsh, hard, sharp, or pressing, but comfortable, gracious, and pleasant), and My burden is light and easy to be borne.
>
> *Matthew 11:28–30*

The Cure for Stress

God's answer to weariness is found in His word. He invites us to study how He lived and learn from His example the best way to handle situations in life. All people grow weary at times.

Watchman Nee, a wonderful Chinese minister, said, "The world is indeed a wearisome place." When we are weary we are exhausted in strength, endurance, vigor, or freshness and we are out of patience and tolerance. Our pleasure in life has been exhausted and we need help. We need to be refreshed not only physically, but mentally and emotionally as well. Being weary is not something to be ashamed of, but it is simply a sign that we need some help or a break.

> Being weary is not something to be ashamed of, but it is simply a sign that we need some help or a break.

The principle I have shared so far of taking time to reward yourself on a regular basis will help you avoid a great deal of weariness. Those little pleasures in life such as a cookie, a pair of shoes, a nap, a walk in the park, a lunch with a friend, a manicure, a bubble bath, or a golf game actually help us more mentally and emotionally than they do physically. When our souls are rested, then our physical strength also increases. Do not fail to take the time to do these little things for yourself because they will help you immensely. But, the first thing we need to do when we feel weary is simply "come to Jesus." Being in His Presence gives us rest and it also provides us with creative ideas on practical ways we can be restored.

Moses had grown weary as he attempted to lead the Israelites from Egypt to the Promised Land and God's word to him was to let others help him (see Exodus 18:18). Sometimes we just need to admit that we need help and that we cannot do everything ourselves. Being needy is not something I was good at in my life and I have had to learn that asking for help is not a sign of weakness, but rather it is wise.

> Moses had grown weary as he attempted to lead the Israelites from Egypt to the Promised Land and God's word to him was to let others help him.

Moses was wearing himself out because he tried to do everything the people wanted him to do and, to be honest, we just cannot keep all of the people happy all of the time and not be worn out ourselves.

God surely knew that we would all need help because He sent us His Holy Spirit, Who is referred to as "The Helper." Go ahead and say it: "I NEED HELP!" Asking is the first rule to receiving, so don't be too prideful to ask for help.

Isaiah said that all people grow weary at times. No matter what our age is or how naturally strong we are, we all have limits and that is OK. It is OK if you cannot do it all. In fact, you can't do it all. Isaiah's instruction was to wait upon the Lord and be refreshed and renewed (see Isa. 40:28–31). Daniel said that Satan actually seeks to wear out the saints of God. We need to remember that: the devil wants us weary, worn out, and exhausted. He will push us until we have no strength left if we are not careful, because he knows that if we are exhausted we will think, say, and do foolish things; we won't enjoy life and our witness to others will not be good.

All of the great men and women of God talked about being weary and how to recover once they became so. We can learn a great lesson from the Prophet Elijah.

Take a Break and Eat a Cake

Elijah was perhaps the greatest prophet in the Bible. God used him to do amazing things and yet we see the human side of Elijah. Elijah (with God's help) made fools of and slaughtered 450 prophets of the heathen idol Baal. They had no machine guns or bombs in Elijah's day, so I suppose he killed them with a sword. Just imagine how tired a person would be if they had a day like Elijah did. Not only did he kill 450 people but he also built an altar, dug a trench, cut a bull in pieces for a sacrifice, got four large jars of water from the well or brook, and repeated this process several times (see 1 Kings 18:21–40). After that he climbed Mount Carmel to pray for rain while his servant looked for rain clouds as an answer to Elijah's prayer to end a three years' drought. When his servant reported that he saw a tiny cloud the size of a man's hand, Elijah told King Ahab (Jezebel's husband) to hitch up his chariot and flee because it was about to rain. Then, after the exhausting day Elijah had already had, the Bible says that "he girded up his loins and ran before Ahab to the entrance of Jezreel [nearly twenty miles] (1 Kings 18:46). He was most assuredly exhausted beyond anything I can imagine when this process was over.

The next day he heard a report that Jezebel had made a vow to kill him the same way he had killed her prophets. Elijah's reaction was that of an exhausted, weary man. He ran into the desert to hide, and he isolated himself from his servants and friends because he was discouraged and depressed. He sat alone in the desert and asked God to take his life (see 1 Kings 19:1–4). Exhaustion can change our personality and make us do things and behave in ways that would not be normal for us. Elijah was normally not afraid of anything. He was very bold. Bold enough to confront and slay 450 of Jezebel's prophets, but now we see him only one day later behaving quite differently. I don't know about you, but I can relate to having days like the one Elijah was having. I have been so tired that exhaustion altered my personality; I have been filled with self-pity and negative thoughts, and I have wanted to isolate myself and have everyone just leave me alone.

Elijah obviously needed help, so God sent an angel to help him, who told him to arise and eat. The angel provided a cake and a bottle of water and told him to eat, drink, and lie down and go to sleep (see 1 Kings 19:5–6). The angel repeated the process again and after that Elijah had strength to go for forty days. Wow! God's answer to the great prophet's exhaustion, weariness, and desperation was *"Take a break and eat a cake."* It was equivalent to *"Eat a cookie and buy the shoes."* I think this is amazing and thrilling because it lets us know that the answer to some of the most difficult times in life is to get some rest, eat something we enjoy, do something we enjoy, take a nap, and keep repeating the process until we feel we can go again.

The multi-billion-dollar stress business might go broke if we all took God's advice on how to cure stress. Perhaps people don't need so many doctor visits, prescriptions, counselors, and treatment centers. Perhaps they just need a vacation for their soul.

I realize that people have serious problems and devastating losses in their lives. I also know that the simple things I am talking about are not the ultimate answer for every situation, but they are the cure for much of the stress that people experience today. Everyone gets weary unless they know how to prevent it, or how to recover.

The Rest of God

In Matthew 11:28–29, Jesus speaks of rest two times. One is the rest of salvation and the other is the rest we need for daily life. The invitation to come to Him and find rest (v. 28) is in reference to receiving salvation through faith in Jesus Christ. When we do that, we find an immediate type of rest that is one we have not experienced previously. We have the rest of knowing that our sins are forgiven and that we are loved and accepted by God. We also have the rest of no longer being afraid of death, because we know that when we die, we will simply pass from this earthly realm into the heavenly realm where we will live eternally in God's Presence.

This first rest is wonderful, but we also need a second rest and Jesus tells us how to have that when He says, "Take My yoke upon you and learn of Me . . . and you will find rest (relief and ease and refreshment and recreation and blessed quiet) for your souls" (v. 29). A yoke is a device that is used to couple two things together, such as the pairing of oxen that were used to pull a plow for farming. It is used metaphorically in the Bible as a reference to submission to authority. It also refers to balancing out a load.[1] If we stay yoked (very close) to Jesus and submit to His authority He will help us balance out our load in life and we will learn how He responds to every situation.

To live a balanced Christian life where the load is not too heavy for us, we must be willing to take up Jesus' yoke in the small things of each day as well as in the big things of life. Some workers find it hard to labor with their fellow workers; some husbands or wives find it hard to endure their in-laws; some employees find it difficult to deal with their boss; students become weary of their relationship with teachers and other students. All of these are things we must bear in life and, of course, we get tired of them. We wish that we could get away from them, or find a way to get them away from us. We may feel cast down, discouraged, depressed, and have no peace, but we must learn that Jesus wants us to be yoked to Him and realize that these things are things we must learn to bear with a good attitude because they are God's portion appointed to us.

God puts different people together and wants us to learn how to love one another and get along peacefully. God may put a careful, tidy person with a careless, messy person. He may put a strong person with a weak one, a healthy one with a sick one, or a clever person with one who is not so clever. He puts hot-tempered, impatient people together with sweet-tempered and patient people. One of them becomes yoked to the other and God uses them to balance one another out. This gives us the opportunity to learn the nature of Christ, and if we struggle against it, we will have no rest. But, if we say to God, "I am willing to take my place; I am willing to obey; I am willing to bloom where I am planted," then we will find rest and joy.

It took me many years to learn that it was useless to try to change something that God had assigned to me as a yoke to bear in life. I had to submit to His will and let Him teach me to be peaceful in the situation. In his book *Balanced Christian Life*, Watchmen Nee said, "The highest life we can live is to welcome all that we may naturally dislike. Let me tell you that you will be filled with the deepest rest within if you will joyfully accept the yoke which God gives you."[2]

God's rest has been available since the seventh day of creation, when God Himself rested. Many things are available today that people fail to enjoy because they are either ignorant of them or because they fail to believe and obey.

> God's rest has been available since the seventh day of creation, when God Himself rested.

Spiritual Rest

Although we need physical rest, the type of rest spoken of in Matthew 11 is spiritual rest. It is a rest of the spirit and soul (mind, will, emotions). It is a rest in work, not from work. When we rest physically, we need to stop working. But this type of rest is different. When Jesus came to Mary and Martha's, he did not chastise Martha for working, but for worrying. He told her that she was anxious and troubled about many things, but that right at that moment, only one thing was needful and that was for her to enjoy His visit. She was concerned about how things looked and was upset that Mary wasn't helping her (see Luke 10:38–41). Martha needed to give herself permission to lighten up! All the things she worried about were not things worth worrying about. The house being perfect wasn't that important, and what Mary was doing was none of Martha's business. She needed to relax and enjoy the miracle of the moment. Jesus had come to her house, and even though she probably needed to make some preparations, she did not need to lose her peace.

Rest is not inactivity, but the harmonious working together of all the faculties and affection—of will, heart, imagination, and conscience. For example, if a person makes a choice to do something that their conscience does not agree with, they will not enjoy the rest of God. Someone just asked me to do something as a favor to them that I did not have peace about doing. If I please my friend by doing what they want me to do then I will not have rest because in my heart I don't really feel it is a right thing for me to do. My actions, heart, mind, and conscience need to work together in harmony. Martha needed to learn to rest while she worked. Martha worked, but in her imagination and thoughts she was angry with Mary because she was not also working and that prevented Martha from being at rest internally while she worked outwardly.

If the emotions, heart, will, or mind is set against the thing being done, there will be no rest. Martha was working, but she resented it so she could not rest. When we have a job to do we should do it willingly, not with resentment. It is vital for us to use our free will and choose the will of God when a thing needs to be done. We say in our heart, "I will do this as a service to God and I will do it with a good attitude."

This is exactly what Jesus did in the Garden of Gethsemane. He knew a job had to be done and that God wanted Him to do it. He prayed about it and even though He was aware that it was going to include unimaginable suffering, He set His will in agreement with His Father's will. He endured the pain and suffering for the joy of the prize that was set before Him. Once He made His decision God sent angels to minister Him. If our attitude is proper we will receive divine help enabling us to do what we need to do.

Change Your Approach to Life

Life will not always change, so we must be willing to change. Ask yourself how you approach each day and situation. Do you have an idea of what you want to take place? Have you already decided that you cannot have rest or joy if you don't get what you want? I hear people say things like, "If it rains tomorrow I am not going to be happy," or, "When I get home from work today I am going to be upset if my children did not clean the house the way I told them to." When we think like this, we are preparing to be upset and lose our rest before we even have a problem. We have made our mind up that we cannot have rest if we don't have our way. We should say instead, "I hope the weather is nice tomorrow, but my joy is within me so I can be happy and have rest in my soul no matter what kind of weather we have." We should think, "I hope the children did what I asked them to do so I don't have to correct them, but I can handle any situation and remain peaceful in my soul."

Do you approach life with a negative, complaining attitude, or with a positive, grateful attitude? Do you take time in life to

> Life will not always change, so we must be willing to change.

reward yourself for your progress, or do you punish yourself for your weaknesses and mistakes? Do you hurry all the time or take the day one thing at a time, asking for the help of the Holy Spirit? Do you live in the now (present moment) or do you live in yesterday and tomorrow in your thinking? How we approach life makes all the difference in our quality of life, so when we can't fix life, let us remember that we can fix our approach to life. Make your mind up that you will be happy if you get your way and you will be happy if you don't.

> Do you hurry all the time or take the day one thing at a time, asking for the help of the Holy Spirit?

We all have endless examples in our life of changing our approach. Dave and I stay in hotels a lot and often find that the bathtub has no stopper to keep the tub filled. I enjoy a bath rather than a shower, so after getting upset numerous times over the lack of a stopper, I decided to carry one with me. It takes up very little space and keeps me in rest. Most hotels don't have very good lighting. I imagine it is because they are trying to save money, but the fact is that most guests don't enjoy being in a dark room. After complaining for years, we now call ahead and ask the hotel for several additional lamps for our room. If the bulbs are not a high enough wattage to put out sufficient light, we go buy brighter light bulbs. Once you get committed to living in rest and peace you will find ways to approach life differently.

Last year we were traveling to Thailand and India and were

stranded in Alaska due to airplane maintenance. I expected to leave St. Louis where it was very cold and end up in Thailand where it was hot, so I left home wearing sandals and didn't take a coat. When we got off the plane in Alaska it was thirteen degrees below zero and the wind was blowing really hard. My daughter-in-law gave me a pair of bright pink socks to put on with sandals (stop and use your imagination); needless to say, they looked ridiculous. I bought a purple fuzzy sweatshirt in the hotel gift shop which I knew I would never wear again and did not want to spend money on, but it was all I could find. So with my hair sticking up because I had been sleeping on the plane, my summer outfit, my pink socks and purple fuzzy sweatshirt, I walked across the hotel lobby quite sure that nobody in Alaska, especially in the middle of the night, would recognize me. But our thoughts are not always God's thoughts, and sure enough the bellman said loudly, "Aren't you Joyce Meyer from television?" Immediately, a few other hotel employees who watch my program came running over, and so we had a small "meet and greet" in Alaska in the middle of the night, with crazy hair, pink socks and sandals, and a purple fuzzy sweatshirt.

I did not want to be in Alaska, and I did not want to run around in the ridiculous outfit I had on, but I only had two choices. I could be upset and lose my rest, which would not change a thing, or I could decide to make an adventure out of it. I chose the adventure and things worked out all right. We can change our quality of life by changing our attitude toward the small and big things that usually irritate and anger us.

Escaping Trouble Is Not the Answer

David prayed that he could fly away from trouble and be at rest (see Ps. 55:5–8), but running from trouble is not the answer. We must face the enemy and defeat him in God's power just as David defeated Goliath. God has given us "going through" power. He has given us a spirit not of fear, but of a calm, well-balanced, disciplined mind (see 2 Tim. 1:7). It is not God's will for us to run or hide from challenges, but to confront them head-on, knowing we can fight a battle and remain at rest. After all, the battle is not ours, but God's!

God never blesses people who run. Wherever they are hiding, He finds them and takes them back to what they ran from so they can face it and experience true freedom. God gives us power and wisdom to deal with situations, not to try to escape them. Avoidance is not a godly character trait.

Elijah tried to run and hide, but God made him go back to the place he ran from and continue the work he had been called to do. After God gave him a cake and a break, He confronted him about his attitude. He asked why he was hiding and what he thought he was doing. Elijah answered out of a bitter attitude and distorted thinking. He said that he alone was left to serve God and people were seeking to kill him. He told God that all the Israelites had forsaken His covenant, destroyed His altars and killed His prophets, and once again Elijah sounded as if he was filled with self-pity as He told God that only he was left being faithful (see 1 Kings 19:9–14). God told Elijah that He had seven thousand prophets left that had not bowed their knee to Baal and He also told him to get back to work. When we don't stay in rest our thinking gets distorted and we lose proper perspective. We want to run away from responsibility, but as we can see with Elijah, God will not allow us to do that because escape is never the answer to life's challenges.

> When we don't stay in rest our thinking gets distorted and we lose proper perspective.

Prayer Precedes Rest

Our first line of defense against discouragement or disappointment is prayer. Pray at the beginning of each day, each project, every trial and disappointment. Don't merely pray for the situation to go away, but instead pray that you will be able to handle the problem, maintain the character of God, and display the fruit of the Holy Spirit. Prayer invites the power of God into our situations. You may recall that earlier in this book we talked about the importance of having revelation concerning the power of God that is available to us who believe. This power can be released through believing prayer.

We are told not to be anxious about anything, but in everything we are to pray and give thanks (see Phil. 4:6). It is foolish and a waste of energy and time to try to do anything before praying. Pray at all times, in every season, with every manner of prayer (see Eph. 6:18). We forfeit more than we can imagine because we often fail to pray.

We will have no rest until we learn to stay calm in every situation (see Ps. 94:12–13). The most foolish thing in the world is to try to do something about something you cannot do anything about. When you are weary and overburdened come to Jesus and find rest. Take His yoke upon you and learn how He handles life, and you will find rest, relief, ease, refreshment, recreation, and blessed quiet for your souls. That sounds like a vacation to me! Do you need a vacation for your soul? If you do, one is being offered to you through learning how to rest your mind, will, and emotions, as well as your physical body.

CHAPTER
12

Priorities

When our priorities are out of order it always creates stress. We need order in our homes, schedules, closets, garages, finances, and everything else in life. God is not the God of confusion! He runs a very orderly universe. There is no chaos in Heaven! God tells us to live in the peace that He left for us, so there must be a way to do it. We have many priorities in life that need attention, but in this book I want to discuss *spiritual priorities*.

Sit, Stand, Walk, and Run

We find all of these words in Scripture. We are told that we are seated in Christ and that refers to us entering the rest of God. We are taught to stand against the devil and all evil. We are to walk in God, walk in love, walk in righteousness, and walk by faith. We are also told to run our race, run to win, and run and not be weary.

We are told to sit, stand, walk, and run, but many Christians try to run without ever having learned and practiced the other steps. These spiritual principles have a proper priority and must be established in our lives in that order. Babies do not jump out of their cribs and begin running around the house. They work a long time at learning to sit with pillows propped around them or with the help of an adult, and after much training and practice they finally learn to sit alone.

> We are told to sit, stand, walk, and run, but many Christians try to run without ever having learned and practiced the other steps.

Some Christians can only stay in rest (seated) if they have other Christians continually propping them up, praying for them, and encouraging them to do so, but we must grow to the place where the rest of God is our normal state and not something we must try to attain. We must learn to sit alone without needing the constant support of others before we can start walking.

I tried to run before I learned to sit and it was disastrous. I felt that I was called to teach other people the word of God so I quickly started a ministry. But I experienced unbelievable stress—so much stress that I was sick and unhappy most of the time. I was trying to run, but I had never learned to sit, stand, or walk yet. Now after more than thirty-three years in ministry I am running fast. I am in the spiritual fast lane, hopefully helping millions of people through the teaching ministry God has given me. I know how to run with God, but I also now know how to sit, stand, and walk in God, and I can do them all simultaneously.

Seated in Christ

The Bible always depicts Christ as being seated after His death, resurrection, and ascension. It says that He ascended on high and sat down at the right hand of Majesty, there to wait for His enemies to be made a footstool for His feet (see Heb. 10:11–13). In other words, Jesus not only did what He was sent to do in rest, but He then entered another dimension of the rest of God to wait for God to do the remainder of what needed to be done. I like to say, "Do your best and God will do the rest."

We must learn to do what is assigned to us from God and never waste time trying to do what only God can do. We cannot go beyond what God has given us grace to do. I can want to change. I can study God's word in areas where I need growth, I can pray about change, but only God can change me. I can do what I can do, but I cannot do what only God can do. Until I learned the difference I lived in stress. I can want a loved one or a friend to live a better life, to be closer to God, or to stop destructive habits. I can pray for them and I can offer help if they will take it, but only God can change them. Saying that we trust God is not hard to do, but true faith enters the rest of God. We do not enter God's rest when we are trying to believe, we enter it when we have believed (see Heb. 4:3, 10). As we talk about rest remember that it is equivalent to being seated! Have you learned how to sit?

Even God rested from His labors of creation and took time to enjoy what He had done. He did what He purposed to do and then He rested. Jesus did what He was sent by God to do and then He rested. Our biggest problem is often that we don't know when we should be finished. When we labor in the flesh without God's help then we have no rest; all we have is frustration and stress.

Each day we have certain purposes that we wish to accomplish and at the end of the day it is proper to rest, not only physically, but our soul also needs a rest. We need rest physically, mentally, emotionally, and spiritually.

We are spiritually seated with Christ in Heaven. Our feet may be on earth, but spiritually we are with Christ in Heaven. Christians live in two realms at the same time. A. W. Tozer said it well: "Our trouble springs from the fact that we who follow Christ inhabit at once two worlds: the spiritual and the natural. As children of Adam, we live our lives on earth subject to the limitations of the flesh and the weaknesses and ills to which human nature is heir. Merely to live among men requires of us years of hard toil and much care and attention to the things of this world. In sharp contrast to this is our life in the Spirit. There we enjoy another and higher kind of life."[1] There we can enjoy the rest of God no matter what is taking place in the natural realm.

Our circumstances on earth don't have to disturb us spiritually if we learn how to stay seated. As believers in Jesus Christ we have had a co-death and co-resurrection with Christ. The Bible says, "We know that our old (unrenewed) self was nailed to the cross with Him in order that [our] body [which is the instrument] of sin might be made ineffective and inactive for evil, that we might no longer be the slaves of sin" (Rom. 6:6).

We are also told in Scripture that "He raised us up together with Him and made us sit down together [giving us joint seating with Him] in the heavenly sphere [by virtue of our being] in

Christ Jesus" (Eph. 2:6). We must learn to identify with Christ and to believe that what He has right now, we also have through our faith in Him. We will not get it at some later date, we have it now (spiritually speaking)! God not only allowed Jesus to shed His blood for the remission of our sins, but He has also put us in Christ so that when the Lord Jesus was crucified God crucified our old man with Him, too. That we were crucified with Christ is a fact in God, but it is impossible for the human mind to explain this fact. That is why we must believe with the heart, rather than trying to reason things out with the mind.

Let us understand that whatever God has done in the past in Christ is always *now* for us. God is the God Who is forever *now*. He is the great "I am!" All the facts in Christ are now and they never pass away, they are forever. The cross of Christ is now, the resurrection of Christ is now, the ascension of Christ is now, the coming of the Holy Spirit is now, and the filling of the Holy Spirit is now. We are seated with Christ now. We must not treat what Christ has done as mere history, but thanks to God all that He has done is forever and it is ours now!

Faith allows us to rest mentally and emotionally. Even our will gets a rest when we have faith in God. We don't worry or reason, we are not upset or downcast, and we are not trying to make something happen that is not God's will—we are at rest! Paul was singing in jail. Jesus was praying for others while being crucified. Joseph decided that if he was going to be a slave, he would be the best slave his owner ever had. He decided that if he was going to be a prisoner (even though he did not commit a crime) that he would be a prisoner with a good attitude.

We need to be honest about what the real cause of our stress is. Is it really our circumstances in life, or is it the way we respond to the circumstances? There is a rest available and we must strive to enter it. Entering the rest of God should be our number one priority after receiving Jesus as our Savior. I ask you again: have you learned to sit and enter God's rest?

Have you learned to sit and enter God's rest?

Learning to Stand in Christ

We can never stand against the enemy (Satan) unless we learn to do it from our first position of being seated in Christ. Rest is a place of power!

> And the God of peace will soon crush
> Satan under your feet.
> *Romans 16:20a*

If we stay calm, God will deliver us. We may say that we are trusting God, but there is no evidence of trust unless we stay seated in Christ.

The Israelites were seriously stressed due to their seemingly impossible situation of being literally between the Red Sea and the Egyptian army! They had no natural way of escape. Yet God told them to hold their peace, remain at rest, and He would fight for them (see Exod. 14:9–14).

Standing is a position of knowing the end from the beginning. We know the word of God and what He has promised, and we choose to believe it more than what we see, feel, or think.

We stand firm in our faith knowing spiritually we are delivered and expecting to see the manifestation of it at any moment. We wait expectantly! We will get weary at times because we usually have to wait longer than we thought we would, but Jesus has said that if we will come to Him any time we feel even slightly weary, He will give us rest. He will give what equates to a spiritual vacation or a vacation for our soul.

Learning to Walk

A walk is made up of many steps, and each one is a choice. Our walk with God refers to how we live our daily life. Once we have learned to sit and stand, we are ready to start taking steps that will eventually enable us to walk. We are not walking with God simply because we attend church or read our Bible. Our walk is about our choices. The Bible says that we should walk (order our lives, conduct, and conversation) in the revealed will of God (see Ps. 119:1). It says that we should walk (order our lives) by what we know to be true (see Phil. 3:16). Knowing truth gives us a responsibility to act upon it. I recently watched a tragic situation unfold as a brother in Christ became entangled in an affair with another woman even though he was married and had two children. The sin of the affair opened him up to all kinds of deception and his situation went from bad to worse as he told many lies and got himself deeper and deeper in trouble. His family was destroyed and he ended up in jail. God used that situation to show me that the more knowledge we have of God and His will the more responsible we are to obey it. When one who truly knows better shows no reverential fear of

God and arrogantly chooses sin, he opens a door in his life that allows the army of hell to march in. Knowing is not enough; we must do and the doing is called our walk with God. We can be in church services ten times a month and still not walk with God. We must walk in obedience.

We are told many times in the Bible to walk in love. Love is merely a word or theory unless it controls actions toward other people. Love can be very mystical unless we understand that at the very foundation of love is daily concern for doing what will benefit others, What will make their lives better and help them?

We are to walk by faith. We live and regulate our lives by our conviction about our relationship with God (see 2 Cor. 5:7). Every action, emotion, and thought becomes subservient to what we believe about God. Enoch walked with God and had continual fellowship with Him, and the Bible says that "he was not, for God took him [home with Him]" (Gen. 5:24). It sounds as if Enoch got so close to God that the world could no longer hold him; he slipped over into the spiritual realm and simply disappeared. The Bible does not say that Enoch died and went to Heaven. It says that he walked so closely with God that he simply was no longer here. Noah walked with God (see Gen. 6:9), Abraham, Isaac, and Jacob walked with God (see Gen. 48:15). They made their personal relationships with God a priority. They sat in God (remained at rest), they stood against their enemies, and they walked with God. They also ran their race and are recorded in the Bible as men of whom the world was not worthy. They made choices and formed habits that they walked in day after day and year after year. We see from the beginning of time men walked with God.

Walking a long way is not difficult if you know when to sit

down awhile and rest. Sometimes your walk is hindered and you need to stand a bit in one place, yet all the while you are making progress. Habakkuk said that when nothing is working right in our circumstances that we can rejoice because God is our Strength, our personal bravery, and our invincible army; He causes us to walk (not stand still in terror, but to walk) and make (spiritual) progress on the high places of trouble, suffering, and responsibility (see Hab. 3:17–19).

> Walking a long way is not difficult if you know when to sit down awhile and rest.

We are instructed to walk in the fear of God, walk as Christ walked, walk worthy of the Divine calling, walk through the valley of the shadow of death, and walk through the fire, the flood, and the storm. Walk in integrity, walk in righteousness, walk in liberty, walk as children of light, and don't walk after the flesh. We can see that walking is a full-time job, so it is no wonder that we must first learn to sit and stand. I am fairly certain that if I make a commitment to walk in all of these areas as God asks me to do, I will occasionally need a vacation for my soul!

Let's Go for a Run

My daughter quite often says to me, "I am going to go for a run today." In the last two years she has become a runner, but she started walking fast and doing a little light jogging long before her trainer let her run. She didn't just decide to run and start running—it doesn't work that way. I tried that method many times and each time I hurt either my feet or my back. My chiropractor finally told me that I was too old to start running now. He may be right about running physically, but I can still run spiritually. However, the same principle of preparation applies in the spiritual realm that applies in the natural realm.

If you have learned to sit, stand, and walk in God, it is time to start running in and with God. David said that he would not merely walk, but run in the ways of God (see Ps. 119:32). Are you ready to run your race with steady, active persistence? Are you ready to be patient and persevere until you reach your goal?

> If you have learned to sit, stand, and walk in God,
> it is time to start running in and with God.

Runners in Paul's day stripped down to a loincloth to prepare for the race. Are you ready to strip off anything that is hindering your run with God? Their bodies were oiled (anointed) for the race. We must live with God in such a way that He can anoint us for service in His kingdom. Runners must be disciplined and focused if they intend to win the race. Deciding to run is a big decision and being successful at it requires a huge commitment.

Are your spiritual priorities in order? If not, this is a good time to make some decisions. God has a race for you to run and His plan is for you to win, but you will have to learn to sit, stand, and walk. You can only win your race if you know how to run with your soul on vacation.

CHAPTER
13

My All in All

The tiny word *all* is used 5,675 times in the Bible, give or take a few depending on what translation you are looking at. It is a small word that means a great deal, and yet we pay so little attention to it. If we read a Scripture that has the word *all* in it and ignore the *all*, it changes the entire context of the Scripture. The word *all* takes us into infinity. Where does *all* stop? How far does it go and what does it include?

Jesus is the Lord of All. Our Al-mighty God, all-sufficient Savior, all blessings flow from Him, and He is all that we need. We frequently say that God is our all, but have we ever stopped to truly understand the impact of that one little word? *All* leaves nothing outside of God's control. As long as we believe that some things are out of God's control we cannot have a proper

> As long as we believe that some things are out of God's control we cannot have a proper soul vacation because there will be something for us to worry about.

soul vacation because there will be something for us to worry about, try to figure out, be upset about, or try to control and change. We will not live life as something to be celebrated because it will keep us worn out all the time. We will probably be intense and unable to relax.

God Knows All Things

God knows all things (see John 21:17)! Don't miss the "all" of that statement. He knows the end from the beginning so He must know everything in the middle. He also has all power, all authority; all things are under His feet, and He fills everything everywhere with Himself (see Matt. 28:18 and Eph. 1:21–23). He sees all, hears all, and is everywhere all the time. If these things are true, then why do we still worry and become anxious? Why do we get emotionally upset when we have a problem or things are not going our way? It must be because we truly don't believe that He has all power, knows all things, and loves us with all of the love that exists in the universe.

How many of our sins does He forgive? Does He forgive some, most, or all? The Bible says that He forgives them all and continually cleanses us from all unrighteousness. It is one those all and forever-now things. When Jesus died on the cross sin was dealt with once and for all, according to Hebrews, and the cleansing goes on continually; it is without interruption and for all time (see 1 John 1:9 and Ps. 103:1–3). God did not put our sins off to the side so He could glance over at them occasionally; they are not in front of Him enabling Him to see them continually; nor did He store them in a box somewhere so He could get them out if need be and remind us of them. He did not cover them up, nor sweep them under a rug, but He has removed them completely (see Ps. 103:12). He has cast all of our sins behind His back (see Isa. 38:17). He is not looking at them and He does not want us to look at them, either.

We don't need to pay for them because that has been taken care of as well. All of our sins have been completely forgiven and there is no longer any sacrifice we need to make. Go back and read that again, please. Did you see the "all" and the "have been"? They have been (not will be) all (not some) forgiven! Jesus atoned for our sins, and that means our account has been reconciled, balanced and we are at one with God. We have peace with God through Jesus Christ. We can live with our soul on vacation and we can celebrate life as it was meant to be celebrated. We can give ourselves permission to lighten up and enjoy God and the life He has provided for us. We don't need to be sad, depressed, and discouraged about our past, not even the past of one moment ago! God does not want us to live life always looking in the rearview mirror. We need not forfeit any joy or enjoyment. With good news such as this, how can we not celebrate?

> All of our sins have been completely forgiven and there is no longer any sacrifice we need to make.

All Things Are Possible

If there are no impossibilities then we can live in constant victory and nothing can threaten us or make us feel afraid of the future. With men a great deal is impossible, but with God *all* things are possible (see Mark 10:27). Everything that is in the will of God will be accomplished in His way and timing.

Is life too much for us? Is there anything that we just cannot handle? Not according to God, for He says through the Apostle Paul that we can do all things through Christ Who is our Strength. We are ready for anything and equal to anything through Him Who infused inner strength into us (see Phil. 4:13).

Before we will let go and let God be our all in all, we usually have to find out the hard way that we cannot do it all. The hard way means that we keep trying and failing over and over until we admit total dependence on God. It can be a long and painful journey and some never reach the end of themselves, but for those who do, it is the beginning of living with their soul on vacation. They know they can't do it all, but they also know that God can and they decide that watching Him do what needs to be done as only He can do will be entertaining. I love to watch God work. It is one of my greatest pleasures in life.

Just how sufficient are we without God? We had nothing to do with being born, no control over our nationality or the color of our skin, and we did not control our ancestry or the basic mental and physical abilities we were born with. A power *no one* understands keeps our heart beating, our lungs taking in air, our blood circulating, and our body temperature up. A simple study of the human body surely must tell us that we have a Divine Creator. What a tragedy to believe that we evolved from apes! A surgeon can cut through human tissue, but, by a miracle no one understands, the body heals itself. We are amazed and impressed by the medicine available today, yet we all grow old and eventually we all die, and no amount of modern medicine can stop that!

Are we self-sufficient? Hardly!

The law of gravity that holds the world together operates independently of us. The balance of oxygen and nitrogen is exactly right for man and animals. The planet is tipped on its axis at exactly 23½ degrees. Were it to vary at all, continents of ice would form at the North and South Poles with a desert in between. If the sun were any farther away we would freeze to death, and if it were any closer, we would die of solar radiation. If the balance of any of these things suddenly changed, even a tiny bit, we would all be instantly destroyed. The Bible says that Jesus is upholding, maintaining, guiding, and propelling the entire universe by His power (see Heb. 1:3). It sounds like a huge job, but He does it without any effort seated (resting) by God's side.

Since we know that God is keeping the universe running properly every second of every day, why would we doubt that He can take care of us? He has all power, all authority, all wisdom, and he loves us with a perfect love that is promised to us unconditionally and forever. Put your faith in Him and enter His rest. Faith is the leaning of the entire human personality on Him in absolute trust and confidence in His power, wisdom, and goodness (see Col. 1:4). Think that over and ask yourself if you trust God absolutely. Are you leaning on Him in every situation? Do you believe that He has the power to help you, and that since He has all wisdom He knows exactly what to do and when to do it? Do you believe that God is good, and that He wants to be good to you? If you do believe these things, then you are ready for the next piece of good news that I have for you.

There Is Nothing for You to Worry About

Worry is totally useless. As I often say, it is like rocking in a rocking chair all day. It keeps you busy, but gets you nowhere. I was a worrier, so I know what a stronghold it can become in our lives. I also know that it is a bad habit that is not easily broken, but since all things are possible with God, then it is possible for us to live free from worry, anxiety, and fear. If you are willing to give up worrying, then you will be able to enter into an attitude of celebration. You can trust God and enjoy life while He solves your problems. Give yourself permission to stop worrying.

> Worry is totally useless. As I often say, it is like rocking in a rocking chair all day. It keeps you busy, but gets you nowhere.

Nothing is outside of God's control, so in reality there is nothing to worry about. If for some reason God could not control a thing, whatever would make us think that we could? When we begin to look at worry in a realistic manner we see how totally useless it is. Our minds revolve endlessly around and around a problem, searching for answers that only God has. We may ponder a thing and ask God for wisdom, but we do not have God's permission to worry. Pondering a thing in God is peaceful, but worry is tormenting. When we worry, we torment ourselves! We can pray and ask God to help us not to worry, but ultimately we must choose to put our thoughts on something other than our problems. A refusal to worry is proof that we trust God and it releases Him to go to work in our behalf.

Worry is a big problem for people. I wonder how much of our mental time is spent worrying, reasoning, and fearing—possibly more than is spent on anything else. Instead of meditating on our problems let's choose to meditate on the "alls" of God. Let us realize how unlimited His power is and trust Him to do what we cannot do.

One relatively short Scripture in the Bible uses the word "all" four times:

Casting the whole of your care [*all* your anxieties, *all* your worries, *all* your concerns, once and for *all*] on Him, for He cares for you affectionately and cares about you watchfully.

1 Peter 5:7 (emphasis mine)

I am asking you to take the time to really look at this verse, word by word, and think about what it really means. We receive revelation through meditation, not just reading quickly. There is great value in digesting a Scripture one word at a time.

Casting means to pitch or throw. So we need to violently refuse to worry—to throw it away! The *whole of our care* means all of our cares. All anxiety, all worry, all concern is to be thrown away, and we should do it thoroughly, once and for all so that we make a decision to never waste one minute of our lives worrying. Not only are we to throw our care away, but this verse says that we are to throw our cares *on God*! Because He is God, He can—and wants to—absorb our cares. What a gift! God *cares for us affectionately*—not begrudgingly. God *enjoys* caring for us. He cares about everything that concerns us and He is always *watching*. Nothing slips by God unnoticed.

Even if we make a firm decision not to worry, worry will present itself to us and try to slip back into our thoughts. Our job is to cast it down the moment we realize it is trying to occupy space in our thinking. I will admit that initially it is quite a battle, but persistence always pays off. The devil will try us to see if we mean business, so we must be firm in our decision. I WILL NOT WASTE ONE MINUTE OF MY LIFE WORRYING! Say it over and over firmly until this new thinking becomes a part of you. When you are tempted to worry, I suggest that you celebrate something God has done for you in the past instead. Remember, the devil hates parties, but God likes them.

Instead of leaning toward the negative and meditating on our problems, let's look for the things in our life that once were problems and have now been solved. We can celebrate those things, and when we do it will increase our faith for current situations to also be solved. Meditating on good things is a decision that you must make and not a feeling you wait to have.

You can order your life according to God's will, rather than allowing it to order you. Remember that God has all power and you are in Him, so you have power, too. You are not a helpless weakling that must put up with any kind of thought that falls into your mind. You have weapons of warfare that will allow you to cast down wrong thoughts and imaginations (see 2 Cor. 10:4–5). These weapons are the word of God being used in various ways. We can sing the word, speak the word, read the word, study the word, and meditate on the word. You can only think about one thing at a time, so the next time you start to worry, just decide to think about something else and go ahead and enjoy your day while God works on your situation.

The next time you start to worry, just decide to think about something else and go ahead and enjoy your day while God works on your situation.

Take a Vacation While You Work

When we learn to live without worrying we can do our work or whatever else we need to do, all the while with our soul on vacation. We can deal with circumstances that are unpleasant and handle all the responsibility we have, and yet remain totally peaceful and calm. I recall sharing this message once in a church, and the pastor of the church got a revelation of what I was saying and literally threw his hands up in the air, slid down into a relaxed position in his seat, and said, "I can pastor this church while my soul is on vacation."

I think those of us who are in leadership feel responsible to make sure everything goes the way it should go. Of course, we should be responsible, but if we take a false or an exaggerated sense of responsibility then we will never enjoy what we do. Casting your care does not mean that you don't care what happens; it just means that you know only God can change it. Your faith is in Him rather than in you, and you can let your mind, emotions, and will rest in Him.

Whatever your assignment is in life, you can enjoy the entire process if you learn how to let your soul (mind, will, emotions) rest. David said, "Be merciful and gracious to me, O God, be merciful and gracious to me, for my soul takes refuge and finds shelter and confidence in you" (Ps. 57:1). David said that his soul (mind, will, emotions) was resting in God. His soul was on vacation! I suggest that you spend some time each morning deciding how you are going to respond to the day. Set your mind to be peaceful no matter what happens.

Our soul needs to be quiet rather than in turmoil. If you take a look at your inner life, what do you see? Are you worried, upset, and stubbornly resisting God's plan, or are you silently waiting on God, expecting Him to be all in all?

> For God alone my soul waits in silence;
> from Him comes my salvation.
> *Psalm 62:1*

How long has it been since you have given your soul a vacation? It is possible to take your physical body on vacation for weeks and yet the entire time never let your soul be on vacation. You can lie on the beach at a beautiful Caribbean island resort while your soul is in turmoil. Your soul needs a vacation possibly even more than your body does. It needs to be quiet and at rest. The entire premise of "eat the cookie...buy the shoes" is designed to let your soul rest. It is not wrong to let go of life's demands and circumstances for a while and do something you enjoy.

It is not wrong to let go of life's demands and circumstances for a while and do something you enjoy.

If we learn to do things God's way, we will be able to work with our soul on vacation and we will be able to vacation without our soul working! One day of inner rest is probably worth more to our overall health than a two-week physical vacation. Give it a try—start practicing letting your mind and emotions rest and while you do it, tell God often that you are trusting Him to supply all of your needs (see Phil. 4:19).

Anytime your soul gets stirred up remind yourself of this Scripture:

> Return to your rest, O my soul, for the Lord
> has dealt bountifully with you.
> *Psalm 116:7*

CHAPTER 14

Give God Your All

When we give God our all we are actually saying to Him, "God, Your will be done and not mine." It is the only way we can live with our soul on vacation. Otherwise, we are always wrestling with something that is not working out the way we want. We exist for God and His glory, and being obedient to His will should be our goal.

> All things were created by and for Him. He existed before all things and in Him, they are all held together. He is the Head of all things and must occupy the first and chief place.
>
> *Colossians 1:16–18*

Is God your Head? Is He your King, your Chief, and does His will rule in your decisions? Have you given God your all? We must answer all these questions honestly, and if we are not able to say yes, yes, and yes—then we need to change.

Jesus said to His Father, "All that is Mine is Yours, and all that is Yours is Mine" (see John 17:10). What a beautiful Scripture!

These thirteen words contain volumes of meaning. What have you not released to God? Whatever it might be is hurting you more than you might realize. Stubbornly hanging onto our own will is never good for us. Anything God tells us to do is always and only for our good if we believe that we will be able to "Let go and let God be God."

I was an expert at being stubborn for more years than I like to admit and perhaps you have been also. But the good news is that we can change! We can surrender and when we do our will goes on vacation. Just last night I had an opportunity to practice what I am preaching. Dave had plans to play golf today, and I might say that it was one of many times that he has played lately. I, on the other hand, have been dutifully working on this book. I asked him if he could play early and get home by three so we could go and eat early. He responded that he wanted to have plenty of time to pray and study before he left for the golf course and that he did not want to have to hurry since it was his last day to play during this trip. I could feel my soul going off of vacation right then and there. I felt words forming in my soul and making their way to my mouth for expression. I said, "You could sacrifice a little; after all, I have been working all week!" I could see right away that kind of approach was not going to work, so I quickly decided to give it to God. I said to Dave, "You make the decision and I will work with whatever works out." In doing this, I was giving God my all, and immediately my soul went back on vacation and God was able to work in Dave's heart. Within less than one minute Dave said, "I will probably be able to get home by three." When I think of the fight we could have had and at one time would have had, I am so glad that I have learned to give it to God. If He can't convince Dave, then I certainly can't. I don't know about your husband, but I have noticed that mine doesn't like to be convinced by me; he wants to think it was his idea. Even if Dave had not changed his mind, it would have done me no good to get upset. He would have still had a good time playing golf and I would have been upset and miserable.

We all have similar situations several times each week, if not daily. How can we live with our soul on vacation if we are going to try to convince God and everyone else to do things our way? We can't, so why not give our all to God so we can experience His all in our lives?

> How can we live with our soul on vacation if we are going to try to convince God and everyone else to do things our way?

I mentioned earlier that one of my greatest joys in life is watching God work. We can either open the door for God to do amazing things through submission to Him, or close the door through being stubborn. My decision to shut up and give the situation with Dave and his golf to God is not so hard now because I have experienced how wonderful it is to live with my soul on vacation. But there was a time when it was one of the most difficult things in the world for me to do. Don't expect that giving God your all will be easy in the beginning. It is easy to say it, but not as easy to do it. Our soul is very much alive—it has strong opinions and thoughts, strong emotions, and a strong will. It wants what it wants, when it wants it. Success-fully turning our soul over to God will be similar to breaking a wild stallion. There will be quite a battle, but you will enjoy the ride when the battle is over.

Satan definitely does not want you to live with your soul on vacation. He wants you to worry, be emotionally upset or downcast, and stubbornly fighting for your own way and resisting the good will of God. Sadly, this is the condition that many Christians are in. They go to church, and sing the song, "I Surrender All," but that is as far as it goes. There is not enough teaching on the soul, and many people don't understand the important role that it plays in our life. The truth is that no matter how long you have been a Christian, if your soul is a mess then you are miserable. The world is already filled with miserable sinners, so we definitely don't need miserable Christians!

Don't Miss God's Best

The Apostle Paul begged those he taught to dedicate all of their members and faculties to God for His will and use (see Rom. 12:1). God will manage if we refuse to do that, because He will find a submitted vessel to work through. But we will miss out on God's best for us.

Why did God choose Noah and his family to be saved in the ark during the flood? What was so special about this one man? The Bible says that Noah did according to *all* that God commanded Him. How much obedience are we willing to walk in? Especially if what God asks us to do makes no sense to our mind or doesn't feel right to our emotions? I doubt that Noah understood what God was asking him to do when he required him to build an ark for an upcoming flood. Noah must have been the laughingstock of his region. I am sure that his obedience hurt his reputation with men. How willing are you to obey God if your obedience is likely to hurt your reputation with men?

Paul said that if he had been trying to be popular with people he would never have become an apostle of the Lord Jesus Christ. We cannot always be God pleasers and people pleasers at the same time.

The Bible doesn't say this, but perhaps Noah was not the first or only man to be invited to build the ark. Maybe God asked others but Noah was the only one willing to obey God. God is not necessarily looking for people with amazing ability, but He searches for availability, and a person who is willing to simply do what He asks them to do. If we will lift our hands to God and say, "I am available to do whatever you want me to do," we can live with our soul on vacation. We will have peace and joy as we journey through life.

The Bible uses some words that we don't hear very often today and I think we should take a look at some of them:

Dedication—Devoted to something, devoted to a divine being, set aside for a special purpose. Are you dedicated to God?

Consecration—Anointed with the Holy Spirit for a special purpose, not to be used for other things, made sacred by a ceremony (see Rom. 1:7 and 1 Peter 2:5).

Do you see yourself as one that is set aside for a special purpose in life?

Sacrifice—Offering something to God by giving up something that we have. We can sacrifice praise, thanksgiving, money, time, or anything that we own. We can also sacrifice ourselves. God wants us to come to Him as a living sacrifice.

Are you willing to make any personal sacrifice to be in God's perfect will?

Submission or *obedience*—Doing what we are asked to do by someone in authority, and with a good attitude.

Are you submissive to God and all other authority in your life?

Chastisement—God's correction (done in love) teaching people to obey Him. Training (often painful) that is intended to develop our character and make us better people.

Do you receive God's chastisement with an attitude of celebration?

Pruning—Cutting back, or cutting off a wild or diseased part of a plant. We are God's plant and He is the Divine Gardener (see John 15:1–2).

How do you respond when God cuts something out of your life that you are fond of?

My experience as a teacher of God's word is that people would normally prefer to hear words such as "love," "grace," "peace," "prosperity," and "blessing." They lose their smiles and become quite somber with words like the ones I've defined above. However, I have discovered that even though they might not clap and cheer while being taught about these words, they will be very happy later on if they learn how to work with the Holy Spirit in applying these disciplines to their lives.

What kind of books do you read? What kind of teaching and preaching do you prefer listening to? Do you have books in your library about character development, integrity, spiritual growth and maturity, going deeper in God, living in God's presence, and obedience to God? Or, do you just read things that make you feel good, but don't confront your behavior or challenge you to change? I could probably go into someone's home and look at their library and tell you what kind of Christian they are and how interested they are in a deeper walk with God.

We offer resource material at our conferences that will help people mature spiritually, but I often hide the meat of the word under "dessert titles," so people will buy them. For example, I have a series on obedience that I call, "How to be radically and outrageously blessed." I have to use the same tactic when I give my dog her medicine. I take the little pill that will keep her out of pain and wrap cheese or turkey around it so she thinks it is a treat. That is the only way to get her to take it.

I once had a teaching series on pride and humility and nobody would buy it because the ones who needed it were too concerned (proud) that someone might see them purchase it and think they needed it. I also tried a series called "Developing Patience," and that did not sell very well either. I actually heard people talking at the resource tables, saying, "You don't want to buy that, you know what happens if you pray for or study patience." They knew that patience is only developed by going through trials, but they didn't want to find out enough to actually begin to work through the process. As I have said before, head knowledge alone is almost useless. The principles of God must be worked into our lives by studying the word and through the guidance of the Holy Spirit. We need what the Apostle Paul called the meat of the word. We need teachings that deal with wrong attitudes, sin, dying to self, and other important lessons.

The Holy Spirit led Jesus into the wilderness, an uncomfortable place where He was tempted by the devil for forty days (see

Luke 4:1–2). Why? So Jesus could put the principles into practice that He had studied and have the experience of resisting and defeating Satan. We don't get any muscle (physical or spiritual) without working out. Any time God leads us into a difficult place it is always for our ultimate good. If you have been avoiding hard places I encourage you to embrace them because they will help you be what God wants you to be.

This Can Be a Turning Point

Perhaps you are being convicted that you have not given your all to God. Well, this can be a turning point in your life. God's will is just a decision away. I would rather start wrong and finish right, than to start right and finish wrong. The Bible is filled with stories of men who started in the will of God, but began drifting from God's will into their own.

> I would rather start wrong and finish right, than to start right and finish wrong.

Saul was anointed by God to be king, and he did some of what God asked him to do, but he did not do all that the Lord told him to do. We must understand the importance of the all. The *all* makes all the difference in the world. *Some* of what God requires doesn't work with Him; it is all or nothing if we truly want to please Him! He is looking for obedience, not sacrifices.

Saul did almost all that God asked, but "almost all" is very deceptive. We can easily deceive ourselves, as Saul did, into thinking we have done what God has asked. Saul had not done God's will and was confronted by the Prophet Samuel. Samuel said, "The Lord sent you on a mission and said, Go, utterly destroy the sinners, the Amalekites; and fight against them until they are consumed. Why then did you not obey the voice of the Lord, but swooped down upon the plunder and did evil in the Lord's sight?" Saul answered Samuel by saying, "Yes, I have obeyed the voice of the Lord and have gone the way which the Lord sent me, and have brought Agag king of Amalek and have utterly destroyed the Amalekites. But the people took from the spoil sheep and oxen, the chief of the things to be utterly destroyed, to sacrifice to the Lord your God in Gilgal" (1 Sam. 15:18–21). It was at this point that Samuel told Saul God did not want sacrifices, but obedience.

If we study this story we can learn a great lesson. First we see that Saul did almost all that God asked, but the little bit he did not do got him into as much trouble as if he had refused to do any of it. Secondly, we can see that Saul deceived himself. His own reasoning denied his conscience its normal and healthy function. I think the worst part of this story is that Saul told Samuel he kept the best of the spoil to sacrifice to God. He said that he disobeyed God in order to benefit God. That is the worst kind of deception!

The worst thing about disobedience is that it promises to make you happy by giving you what you want, but it ends up making you miserable. We can never be truly happy with anything less than God's perfect will. I have heard people speak on the permissive will of God and say that God wants us to walk in His perfect will, but that there is a place called God's permissive will that is somewhere between being out of God's will completely and being in His perfect will. I suppose that means something God will put up with, but doesn't approve of.

I personally don't like that kind of teaching, because I believe as a teacher of God's word that it is my job to help people be excellent, not mediocre. I realize that we may spend most of life working toward being in the perfect will of God, but we should definitely hunger for it, crave it, pursue and go after it with all of our might. Let's not be mediocre people, who settle somewhere in the middle, halfway between God's worst and His best. I can't think of a good name for that place, but I suppose we can just call it a mess and be fairly accurate.

Saul started out good, but he drifted fairly quickly into doing his own thing. Jacob, on the other hand, started really bad and ended up good. Jacob was a man who cheated, lied, tricked people, and connived to get what he wanted, but eventually he gave his all to God and became a great servant of God. In Genesis 32:22–28 you can read about how Jacob was restored to God after he was willing to give up all that he had in order to have peace in his soul. His soul definitely needed a vacation. He had spent his life running and hiding, worrying about being caught and punished for his deceptive behavior. But he decided to change. It is never too late to do things right! This can be a turning point for you if you need one.

Is Your Behavior Pleasing to God?

I established earlier in the book that God is pleased with us as His children. He loves and accepts us as we are, but if our hearts are right toward Him, then we will also want to please Him in all things. Is God pleased with how you dress, how you spend your money, what your entertainment choices are, what you read, watch, and talk about? It is true that God loves us no matter what choice we make, but He also said that if we loved Him we would obey Him (see John 14:15). Total consecration is definitely a journey, but the question is, where are you headed? Do you want God's perfect will enough to sacrifice anything in order to have it? Are you willing to give God your all?

Jesus once asked a rich, young ruler to give all of his money to the poor, and the young man went away sad because he was unable to give his possessions (see Matt. 19:21–22). Jesus would have given it back to him many times over with joy, but the young man failed his test. He kept his possessions, but he had no joy. Sadly, much of the world is in the same condition as the young man. People's possessions end up between them and God, and, sadly, their possessions are more important to them than they should be. Those people stubbornly hang onto their ways and willfulness, refusing to submit to God; they end up sad, depressed, angry, and unable to maintain good relationships. They are forever looking for something to fill the void in their souls.

Oh, if people only knew the beauty of living with their souls on vacation. Give your will a vacation by submitting it to God and start celebrating life. Stop wrestling with God, and you will stop going around and around the same mountains (problems) because you are determined to have your own way.

> Give your will a vacation by submitting it to God and
> start celebrating life.

What does the richest man in the world have if his money is gone? What does the most famous movie star or singer have if something happens and they lose their ability to perform? What does the most beautiful woman in the world have when she grows old and her skin is wrinkled, her hair is gray, and she is perhaps walking with a walker? We must make decisions now that we will be happy with later on in life, because later on always comes. I want to give my all to God so I never have regrets later on about what could have been if I had obeyed.

When we give our *all* to God, when we obey Him in *all* things, and when *all* of our confidence is in Him, and when we only want what He wants us to have, there is nothing left to the soul but peace and rest (vacation). We have discovered the resurrection life that Paul talked about that lifts us out from among the dead while we are still in the body. The Psalmist talked about being hidden in the secret place of the Most High (see Ps. 91:1). I believe we have found that place when we know that from Him and through Him and to Him are *all* things. For *all* things originate with Him, live through Him, center in Him, and end in Him (see Rom. 11:36).

Are you tired and weary, overburdened and exhausted? Then come to Jesus and He will give you a vacation for your soul! Your mind, emotions, and will can all be at rest and you can be a Christian that is an alleluia from head to foot, as Augustine of Hippo said you should be.

15

Celebrate Discipline

Living with our soul on vacation will require discipline. On the surface, that sounds like a contradiction. But we will need to use discipline in our thoughts, our emotions, and our willingness to release our will to God's will. If we are going to give up worry, upset, and stubbornness, and instead choose to celebrate, party, eat cookies, buy shoes, play games, and have feasts that last several days at a time, won't we eventually get into trouble? Yes, we would if we had no balance. That's why we need to understand the role discipline must play in all areas of life. Usually people grimace and groan when they hear the word "discipline," but discipline is not our enemy. In fact, it is actually our very good friend. Discipline helps us to be what we say we want to be and have what we say we want to have, but never will have without it. God has given us a spirit of discipline and self-control according to Scripture (see 2 Tim. 1:7). Self-control is one of the fruits of the Spirit-led life. A life without discipline is a disaster, and one that is all discipline and no celebration is a dry desert. We must have balance!

As we learn to celebrate other things, let us also learn to celebrate discipline, because it is a wonderful tool that God has given us to be our helper, not our master. When various disciplines become laws, they become the master and we are the slaves. For example: When I was a young mother and homemaker, I was extremely disciplined about my housework. I cleaned house every day and that included dusting, polishing, sweeping, and using the vacuum cleaner. Of course the dishes were never in the sink for long, and the laundry was done daily. I refused to do anything that could have even hinted of entertainment until all of my work was done. I was proud of myself and actually looked down on my less-disciplined friends.

> Let us also learn to celebrate discipline, because it is a wonderful tool that God has given us to be our helper, not our master.

As I grew in my relationship with God and started learning to be led by the Holy Spirit, I had a day when some friends invited me to go shopping with them and I not only had a desire to go, but felt the Holy Spirit telling me to go. However, I said no, because my disciplined routine had become a law for me that I lived by. I never deviated from it—I got all my work done before anything else! I ended up having a miserable day. I resented the fact that I was working and my friends were enjoying themselves, but I failed to see that it was my fault. Nothing went right that day because I was being led by Joyce, not God.

As a child I realized that I did not get corrected by my dad when I was working, only when I was playing or laughing too loud. It seemed to me that the world applauded work, but disdained play. I felt safe when I was working and following the rules. Thankfully, I eventually learned that although disciplines are necessary, we must not let them rule us. It is permissible to occasionally say, "I just cannot do that discipline today...I have to play!" God had to teach me that the dirt would still be around the next day and that like Martha, I was often overly anxious and worried about things that I didn't need to be concerned with. We all need some Mary days. Days when we lighten up and give ourselves a break!

Occasionally we just cannot go to the gym, or stay on our diet, or clean house, or do whatever our routine is, and that is not wrong as long as we also have the discipline to get back on track the next day. The problem comes in when we have more undisciplined days than we do ones that are disciplined. Israel was commanded by God to have feasts, parties, and celebrations several times a year, but they were also commanded to work more than they partied. God said that in six days He created the world and rested on the seventh, and He gave us the same formula.

I eat a cookie (with icing) approximately once a week, but I know that I cannot eat one daily and not have a bad result. Sadly, some people cannot do things in moderation. They say, "I am an all-or-nothing person." But I don't believe that is the way God intended us to be. I have had people tell me that if they allow themselves to eat one cookie, they will end up eating another and another and another, so they have to deny themselves all the time. They also tell me how sorry they feel for themselves that everyone else can enjoy a dessert now and then and they can't. I believe the devil has deceived them and they have forgotten that God has given them a spirit of discipline and self-control. You can say yes when you want to and no when you want to. You have the same power in you that raised Christ from the dead!!!!!

Develop a New Image

How you see yourself is your image of you. It is like a picture you carry in your mental wallet and it affects all of your words, emotions, actions, and decisions. If you see yourself as someone who cannot control themselves, then that is the way you will be. If you see yourself as a person who has discipline and self-control then you will manifest discipline and self-control.

In God's kingdom things work differently than they do according to the world's ways. For example, God's word teaches us to line our thinking up with His, and then what He says will come to pass (Proverbs 23:7). That is the opposite of how the average person who has no knowledge of godly ways functions. They only believe what they see. They have no knowledge of or belief in the spiritual realm. As Christians, we believe first and then see! We trust God's word and promises more than we trust how we feel or what we see with our natural eyes.

If God says that we have a spirit of discipline and self-control then we need to think and say that we have a spirit of discipline and self-control. If you will see yourself the way He sees you (finished) then you will become what He says you are. We must remember that God sees the end from the beginning. He called Abraham a father of many nations long before he had a child. He calls us disciplined and self-controlled and we must have that godly image if we want a life of freedom.

Discipline Is Freedom

How do you view discipline? Do you see it as something that controls you, or something that helps you control yourself? Do you see it as something you *have* to do, or something that helps you become the person you truly want to be? Living a disciplined life is the only pathway to freedom. Discipline is not bondage—it is freedom!

Disciplining ourselves to exercise and develop good eating habits sets us free to feel good and be comfortable in our clothes. Disciplining ourselves to manage our money wisely sets us free from the pressure of need and debt. Disciplining ourselves to be excellent rather than mediocre or downright lazy gives us the enjoyment of self-respect. Discipline is hard work, but it is easier than trying to live a life that is out of control.

Discipline allows us to enjoy a clean, well-kept home, automobile, and work space. In many ways it sets us free from fear. We don't have to fear an economic downturn if we have disciplined ourselves to be prepared spiritually and financially. Discipline and self-control are both gifts from God and are intended to help us enjoy the good life that is God's will for us.

This book is about enjoying the freedom of celebration. It is about giving yourself a break and rewarding yourself for progress. It is about recess and vacation, but the truth is that none of those freedoms are possible unless we also use discipline and self-control. Using a generous amount of discipline and self-control is what makes a life of celebration possible. I would be doing you an injustice if I gave you the idea that you can do nothing but party, feast, and celebrate. Actually, even if we could do that we would not enjoy it because God has built us to need balance. We actually need the discipline as well as the party. We might even say that the discipline is what gives us the right to the party.

> Using a generous amount of discipline and self-control is what makes a life of celebration possible.

You might remember that I wanted to eat the cookie *after* I had done four sessions in my conference and had one more to go. I had studied, prayed, worked, and disciplined myself and was in need of a reward. I like my occasional cookie, but I discipline myself to a strict eating plan and three workouts per week at the gym. I like to buy shoes, but I discipline myself to give shoes away and I discipline myself to be able to pay for my shoes. I don't put them on a credit card having no idea how I will pay when the bill comes in.

About now you may be thinking that you liked the first few chapters of this book better than you do this one, but be courageous and keep reading. If you quit now without learning the importance of discipline you will never be able to truly enjoy the other liberties I have discussed.

Inner Disciplines

Richard J. Foster in his wonderful book called *Celebration of Discipline* teaches about the importance of inner disciplines, which are really spiritual disciplines. I want to talk about them also because without inner discipline we will never have outer discipline. For example, if I don't discipline myself to study God's word and pray, I will probably never use wisdom with my words. I won't understand the importance or power of my words if I don't know God's word. If we don't know God then how can we know anything about what is right and wrong, wise or foolish? How can we know without studying that He is the way, the truth, and the life (see John 14:6)? If we don't know God's principles of wisdom then it is easy to live with financial pressure simply because we are controlled by emotions when we make purchases. We can spend our entire lives in selfish self-centeredness and never even understand that it is the root cause of most of our problems.

Richard Foster said, "Superficiality is the curse of our age. The doctrine of instant satisfaction is a primary problem. The desperate need today is not for a greater number of intelligent people, or gifted people, but for deep people."[1]

Jesus challenged His disciples to come out into the deep to find what they truly desired (see Luke 5:4).

In order to live the deeper life we must learn to discipline thoughts, attitudes, and emotions. We must learn the disciplines of prayer, worship, Bible study, meditation, fasting, giving, service, submission, solitude, and many other things. Living a shallow life is equivalent to living according to our own thoughts, feelings, and will. The Bible refers to it as carnality, or living according to the flesh. The deeper life is enjoyed by a person who has learned the art of discipline. They learn to discipline the inner life and the outer life as well. As I disciplined myself to spend time with God daily in solitude, reading, and prayer (conversation with God), I received strength from God to be able to discipline my outer life (mind, will, and emotions).

Applying discipline has set me free to enjoy a life where I am not controlled by an unexpected and uninvited emotional downturn due to difficult circumstances that came without an invitation. Discipline sets me free from raging against an unexpected hormone that decided to go in the wrong direction without any warning. I no longer have to bow to negative thoughts, ideas, and imaginings that don't agree with God's word. But, I would not have known God's word had I not disciplined myself to learn it. So we can plainly see that the discipline of the inner spiritual life is the doorway to being able to discipline the other areas of our life.

Spiritual disciplines are intended for ordinary human beings and not just for the spiritual giants or those who hold some type of ministry position. They are for moms and dads who go to work, clean house, cut the grass, buy groceries, and do their best to raise their children. They are for boys and girls, teenagers, young singles, and not-so-young singles. Don't be deceived into thinking that you are not one of the elite called to a deep spiritual life. Christ has broken down all of the dividing walls and we are all the same in Him. We all have the same responsibility and the same privileges. If you think this deeper life is not for you then you won't try to attain it and that would be tragic indeed.

You need no special training to be deeply spiritual except that you are hungry for more of God in your life. There must be a longing in your soul for a genuine experience with God. Without that longing, you will always be satisfied with counterfeits and mirages. You might think that an occasional good time is the best you can have, but in reality you can have joy that cannot be explained. To become deeply spiritual does not mean that you must wear all black, wipe the smile from your face, and maintain a look of intensity at all times. Deeply spiritual people are the happiest and most peaceful people on earth.

Legalistic, rigid people are miserable, but when discipline is practiced under the leadership of the Holy Spirit, it is one of the most beautiful tools God has given to man. And the result of that discipline is grace, flexibility, peace, and joy.

It is possible to be overly disciplined, as I once was. Richard J. Foster said, "The Spiritual Disciplines are intended for our good. They are meant to bring the abundance of God into our lives. It is possible, however, to turn them into another set of soul-killing laws. Law-bound Disciplines breathe death."[2]

We may become zealous in our quest for spiritual disciplines and merely turn them into external rules that never change the heart. The Pharisees were the most disciplined men of their day and yet they were sad-faced, rigid, and critical. They told everyone what to do because they knew what was right, but they personally had no spiritual tenderness. They never lifted a finger to help anyone! True spiritual disciplines should make us more like Jesus, Who is humble, gentle, meek, and lowly, and yet at the same time is mighty, powerful, and a victorious warrior. Jesus always maintains the perfect balance in everything.

Disciplines are not meant to manipulate and control you. They are intended to keep you on the narrow path that leads to life (see Matt. 7:13–14). You can be deeply spiritual and amazingly disciplined, and yet celebrate every day that God gives you on earth. You can be deeply spiritual and laugh four hundred times daily like little children do.

Discipline Yourself

One of the most irritating things in the world to me is a person who is extremely disciplined in some area of their life, and who tries to force their discipline on me. We must beware of trying to make everyone do what we do. Even if it would be good for them, it is between them and God. It is best to pray for people (humbly) and not offer advice unless they ask for it or it is evident that God is opening a door for us to make a suggestion. I have had to remember that God has given me *self*-control, and that means I am supposed to control myself, not others. I need to discipline myself before I even think about trying to help anyone else.

When we have developed a discipline in a specific area we often try to convince other people that they need to discipline themselves in the same way we do. Some people who don't drink coffee like to try and make me feel guilty when I drink it, but they are wasting their time. I already gave it up and did not feel any different than I do when I drink it. I have also had discussions with the Lord about it and checked with a nutritionist who assures me that in moderation caffeine is not bad for me. Just because God has led someone else not to drink caffeine does not mean that He is leading me that way. My husband tried to talk me into exercising for years, but it did no good until God told me to do it. On my cookie day, I hate being with one of *those people* who never eats sugar—I don't want to feel their thoughts and see their disapproving looks about what they may assume is a lack of discipline on my part.

I had a bad habit for many years of trying to tell others what to do in areas where I was successful, but I finally learned that

God told me to discipline myself, not everyone else. I believe
we often lose our own victories through trying to give advice to
others. Be careful when you think you stand, lest you fall (see
1 Cor. 10:12). Trying to tell others what to do is often a manifestation of pride and it always opens the door for a fall. One of the
secrets to being successful is to keep your success to yourself.
When I am trying to lose a few pounds I invariably cannot stick
to my plan if I start telling everyone what I am doing. However,
if I keep it mainly between me and God, then He strengthens
me and gives me success.

> I had a bad habit for many years of trying to tell others what
> to do in areas where I was successful, but I finally learned
> that God told me to discipline myself, not everyone else.

There is a time to share things, but also a time to be quiet.
You have a spirit of discipline and self-control, and it is your
best friend if you know how to use it properly. It will help you
be deeply spiritual and successful in all areas of life. We should
definitely celebrate discipline.

Some Practical Guidelines

If you have lots of areas in your life that you realize need discipline, don't try to correct all of them at once. "One thing at a
time" is usually the best policy. Pray, asking God to give you
direction about what to tackle first, and when you believe you
have a proper goal then get a realistic plan on how to accomplish

it. Notice I said pray first and then plan. Don't make your own plan and tell God He has to make it work. I also want you to notice that I said make a *realistic* plan.

If you need to clean your basement and garage, don't plan to get them both cleaned in one day. It might be better to set a goal of two weeks. It is always better to reach your goal early than it is to have unreasonable expectations, get discouraged, and never reach it at all. Perhaps you should dedicate one or two hours a day to the project until it is finished. Once you reach the goal you can check it off your list, look at the finished product with joy, and eat a cookie!

Maybe you need to lose fifty pounds and you would like it gone two months before swimming season begins and you want to wear a bathing suit. That probably won't happen! If that is your goal you won't last long because you will have defeated yourself with an unrealistic goal. Maybe you should say, "By this time next year I will have lost fifty pounds, I will look great in my bathing suit, and I will be exercising regularly." That is the long-term goal and you can set short-term goals that will help you reach it.

Maybe your goal should be to lose six to eight pounds each month. I know that doesn't sound like much, but usually weight that is lost slowly and properly is more likely to stay off than weight lost through an unhealthy fad diet of some sort. The more overweight you are, the faster you will lose weight, so this goal must be an individual one, but it should be realistic.

You will always have something in life that you are working toward. You will never have everything checked off your list. So keep at it and enjoy the journey. I can remember when I felt very disappointed with myself if I ran out of day before I got everything accomplished that I had planned. It seemed that I was always dissatisfied with my progress until I finally realized that no matter how much I did there would always be new things coming up. I can check one thing off of my list, but another one is being added, so with God's help I finally learned to do my best each day and get up the next day and start again (with a good attitude).

> You will always have something in life that you are working toward. You will never have everything checked off your list. So keep at it and enjoy the journey.

As we try to reach our goals we will have times of success and we will also have times when we feel that we failed. But, the truth is we never fail unless we quit and give up. I love John Maxwell's theory that we can fail forward.[3] In other words, we can learn from our mistakes and keep pressing on. If you are on a diet and suddenly on the tenth day you get emotional and eat everything in sight, that doesn't mean that you should just give up and keep overeating every day. See the eating day as a momentary setback in a long-range plan, get up the next day, and keep going in the right direction. Messing up one day doesn't need to ruin your entire plan if you don't let it.

If you are trying to get out of debt and have been really disciplining yourself and cutting back on unnecessary spending, then you really blow it and buy something that you should not have bought, don't give up. Perhaps you can return the item, but if you can't then learn a good lesson and keep on going forward. Even a turtle will eventually get where he is going!

I think my best practical advice is to realize that our lives don't get out of order in one day, and they won't get back in order in one day. If we want success we need to realize that it won't come quickly or be maintained without an effort. We are usually undisciplined for quite a while in an area before it begins to catch up with us and once we decide to do what is right it will take time to start seeing results. Be committed to a lifestyle of discipline and self-control. Don't have an attitude that says, "I want to hurry up and lose this excess weight so I can eat whatever I want to again." If that is your attitude you will live on a roller coaster of ups and downs all of your life. Make a decision that you are going to live a disciplined and self-controlled life, but that along the way you will give yourself an occasional break to eat the cookie and buy the shoes, or whatever it is you enjoy doing.

And last, but not least, I want to suggest that in addition to planning your disciplines for the day you also plan something that you enjoy. Take time for recess! Make that latte and enjoy drinking it, take a walk in the park; if you are going to make it a cookie day, be sure to enjoy every bite. I have found that I don't discipline myself without a plan and I have also found that I am more likely to do things I enjoy if I plan them, too.

> Take time for recess! Make that latte and enjoy drinking it, take a walk in the park; if you are going to make it a cookie day, be sure to enjoy every bite.

God has given us a spirit of discipline and self-control and all we need to do is exercise it. By the way...the more you discipline yourself the easier it will be!

CHAPTER

16

Discipline Yourself to Celebrate

The theme of this book has been celebration and learning to reward ourselves for progress. It has been about giving yourself permission to lighten up and not be so intense. I want you to celebrate life and enjoy it immensely because I believe that is God's will. Since life can often be challenging and we can easily get entangled in all of its problems, we will need to actually discipline ourselves to keep the theme of celebration alive. We all have to deal with problems that arise and people that frustrate and/or disappoint us. There is no way to be alive and avoid that, but if we add generous portions of celebration to our lives we will find that we don't feel so overwhelmed by the unpleasant parts. Remember that Jesus said we should come to Him when we feel overburdened and worn out and He would give us recreation for our souls (see Matt. 11:28–29).

I want to emphasize again that when you plan your day, make sure to make room for something that you enjoy. If you are not accustomed to doing this, and most of you probably aren't, it will require discipline. I can almost guarantee you that initially you will feel guilty simply because we feel more acceptable when we are working and accomplishing something. I surveyed a room full of people yesterday and asked if they felt better about themselves when they were working or relaxing. All of them said they felt more acceptable when they were working. They all happened to be young mothers and confessed that they felt guilty relaxing if any work remained to be done. Why do we feel that way? I think the correct answer is comprised of several parts. First, we are created by God to be responsible and that is a necessary and a good trait. However, if we let the good thing go too far it becomes a bad thing, and we become overly responsible to the point that we cannot relax. We can easily take on a false sense of responsibility where we feel responsible to do more than is reasonable. We can join the driven society around us that is supporting a multi-billion-dollar stress-related business, or we can discipline ourselves to include regular celebration and rewards for progress. The fact that our entire society seems to be driven, and worships career success, becomes another part of the reason why most people feel guilty if they are not accomplishing something all of the time.

I have met young moms who feel they are not what they should be unless they can juggle marriage, parenting, homemaking, and a career. I remember when it was out of the ordinary for a mother to work outside of the home, and now it seems to be rare if they don't. What each family decides to do is their choice, but one thing is for sure: no mother should feel belittled because she decides to devote herself entirely to her family and make that her career. One thing we don't have to do is drive ourselves to be like someone else. Jesus set us entirely free from the tyranny of comparison and competition, and we can and should celebrate that we are unique (see 2 Cor. 10:12).

Constantly Making Adjustments

As you add celebration to your life you may find that you occasionally go too far and need to make adjustments. One of the reasons I had so much trouble not working all of the time is that for some reason I was afraid I might get lazy if I lightened up. My family laughed at me when I told them that, but it is the truth. I know that it is easy to go too far in anything, and I just want to make sure that I stay in balance. I have learned to trust God with the whole thing and simply follow the leading of the Holy Spirit. I work hard, but I rest. And when I have rested and celebrated enough then I go back to work.

There are people who don't like to work, and they have no problem at all partying and playing all of the time, but that is not true celebrating because they are not doing anything to be celebrated. Celebrating nothing is not genuine celebration! These individuals are lazy and undisciplined and quite often their natural temperament tends toward fun, but they have never learned the discipline and reward of hard work. I think we will all be out of balance in some way if we don't continually make adjustments.

I am more naturally inclined toward work, accomplishment, and responsibility; therefore I have had to learn how to discipline myself to rest, celebrate, and take time to reward myself for progress. It was not an easy lesson for me to learn, because the other traits were deeply ingrained in me and had become who I was. I was not a human *being*, but instead I had become a human *doing*. I also know people who have struggled just as much as I did trying to overcome the tendency to play too much. They were undisciplined people who found work and responsibility hard to deal with. They were experts at procrastination and avoidance, but they have asked for God's help and used principles of discipline to overcome excess in their area just as I did in mine. The bottom line is that we all have to discipline ourselves; otherwise our lives will be out of balance.

I have found that I rarely make a decision to fix something without eventually needing to make more adjustments. I will probably always have to stand fast in this liberty of not working all the time and taking time to celebrate. I think some people will always have to discipline themselves to not play too much and do the work that needs to be done. I am always making adjustments and I find that most well-balanced people do the same thing. It is simply too easy in our society to get out of balance. We live in a driven society where pushing ourselves is applauded, yet we also live in a society that is addicted to entertainment, so we should always exercise ourselves to find the right balance between the two opposite extremes.

> We should always exercise ourselves to find the right balance between the two opposite extremes.

I regularly notice that I have gotten out of balance in some area of my life and have to make an adjustment. I work hard to maintain good eating habits, but several times a year I start eating too much of something (usually cookies) and have to have a meeting with myself and set new goals again! There was a time when I felt like a failure when that happened, but I have learned that I can fail forward. I can simply realize I am out of balance and start doing the right thing again. It would be better if I never got off track, but I am a human and won't manifest perfect control in every area every day of my life. God has given us a spirit of discipline and self-control so we can get back on track when we notice that we have veered off. He also gives us His Holy Spirit to make us aware of those times and help us make the adjustments needed. You are living a self-defeating life if you feel guilty each time you realize you need to change something. As I said earlier in the book, we can and should celebrate being convicted by the Holy Spirit about areas in our life that need to change. We can celebrate that we have the ability to stay in balance by making regular adjustments to our lifestyle.

We can take a negative view and moan over the fact that we need to change, or we can celebrate the fact that we can change with God's help. That is good news! I love good news—it is like water to a thirsty soul (see Prov. 25:25). We will be changing all of our lives. If we don't need to change anymore that means we are dead. Life is about progress and progress is about change, so if you don't like change you will have to get over it.

Facing Truth

Truth is something we need to celebrate because we cannot change anything until we face truth about where we are. And that is usually the hardest part. Neither can we change until we stop feeling guilty about where we are right now. The process of conviction, facing truth, and disciplining ourselves to change goes something like this:

I am eating too much but I don't want to face it, so I keep making excuses. I say things like: "I don't eat as much as most people that I know," or "The older I get the slower my metabolism works," or "The dry cleaner must have shrunk my pants." This year when I got out my summer pants I noticed they were all tighter. Since I had needed to have some of them taken in the year before last, I was sure that the seamstress took them in too much and I just didn't notice it last year. My point is that our excuses are endless. They are actually reasons stuffed with lies. The next phase for me is to face the truth that I am eating too much. If you come to this point you might even want to say it out loud or confess it to a friend: "I have been eating too much and that is why I have gained weight." The truth will set you free.

For me I find that writing down *everything* I eat for two weeks helps me get back on track. First of all I tend not to overeat if I have to write it down and look at my list, and secondly I start realizing how excessive I have become when I begin to say no to things so that I don't have to write them down.

Once I have faced the truth and fully realized what I did that caused my problem, it is not that difficult to fix it. I am usually a little hungry for about three days, but I can even avoid that by nibbling on carrots and celery. Before long I am back to my perfect weight, I feel good about the way my clothes fit, and I feel good because I am disciplining myself. Then I can have my days of celebration (cookie days) without a gnawing feeling that I am doing the wrong thing. I have just gone through one of my adjustment times while writing this book and I am celebrating the fact that I can see the truth, receive conviction, and with God's help make the changes I need to make. Jesus came to bring good news and part of that good news is that we can find a way to celebrate everything if we will look for it.

Refuse to Live in Mourning

Part of disciplining ourselves to celebrate life is refusing to live in mourning. There is a time to mourn, but we dare not let it become a way of life. The Bible says that weeping (mourning) endures for a night, but joy comes in the morning (see Ps. 30:5). There are things that happen in life that rightfully need to be mourned over, but joy always returns to balance things out. We must let the joy back into our lives after times of sadness and not feel guilty about enjoying life after disappointment or even tragedy has struck. There is a time to mourn and a time to rejoice, but we must not live in the state of mourning.

Part of life is dealing properly with sadness and disappointment. We cannot avoid them—and we should not deny the emotions that go with loss of any kind—but we *can* recover! I was saddened when I learned that a trusted employee had been stealing from us, but I rejoiced that God brought the wrongdoing into the light and it was discovered. I have a time of mourning when people I love die, but I can also rejoice that they knew Jesus and are spending eternity with Him. I am sad when I realize that I have let an area of my life get out of balance through lack of discipline, but I can rejoice that I now see the truth and am back on track. For all mourning there is an offsetting reason to celebrate, and although mourning is proper and is even part of our healing, it cannot last forever. We cannot live in a state of mourning over things that have happened that we cannot change. In Christ there is always a place of new beginnings and that is good news worth celebrating.

> In Christ there is always a place of new beginnings and that is good news worth celebrating.

We prolong our tragedies by continuing to mourn over them long after they are over. We can easily make the mistake of regretting what we have lost instead of counting what we have left and moving forward. I lost my childhood and my innocence through abuse, and it was tragic indeed. Even though I got away from the abusive situation at the age of eighteen, I continued to mourn and live in regret and bitterness for approximately another thirty years. It was only after I had been taught by the Holy Spirit the principles I am sharing with you in this book that I understood the importance of refusing to mourn any longer. It was a decision I had to make based on God's promise of a new life made available to me in Jesus.

We see this principle brought out beautifully in the book of Esther. The Jewish people were being oppressed and threatened with extinction, but God delivered them. As soon as the deliverance was secured, they were instructed to mourn no more, but to declare a holiday during which they would rest, feast, be glad, and send gifts to the poor. They were also instructed to keep this holiday every year so they would remember the time when they got rest from their enemies, and as the month that their sorrow was turned to gladness, and from mourning (Esther 9:18–22).

They had not only been physically delivered, but they chose not to continue thinking and talking about the past tragedy. I had to do the same thing in order to truly be free. I walked away from abuse at the age of eighteen, but continued it in my soul for another thirty years. My soul needed a vacation but I did not even know one was available. Thank God for revelation and the truth that sets us free. Once we know it, we can discipline ourselves to act accordingly and enjoy the benefits of knowing and serving God. God says to rejoice and celebrate and we must discipline ourselves to do it.

I pray that as I share these things with you that they will help you avoid wasting years of your life in mourning as I did. Hopefully you can benefit from them at a younger age than I did, but whatever your age is, rejoice that you see the light now and can start celebrating today. Even if you don't "feel" like celebrating, you can discipline yourself to do it and your feelings will eventually catch up with your decision.

I Can't Celebrate... I Still Have My Problem!

Perhaps you still have your problem and have not yet been delivered as Esther and her people were. You may be thinking that you can't celebrate because there is nothing to celebrate yet, but you can begin by faith because you have your hope in God.

The Psalmist David gives us a good example of this in the Psalms. He talked to his own soul and asked it why it was mourning because of his enemies and why it was cast down? He then instructed his own soul to put its hope in God and wait expectantly in God Who was the help of his countenance (see

Ps. 42:9–11). Our countenance is the look we have on our face, so David was actually saying that God could help him smile even in the midst of his unpleasant circumstances. I have found that talking to myself (my soul) is often very helpful. We dare not let our emotions control our actions. If we do then we are letting the devil and our flesh control us rather than the Holy Spirit. David realized that he was sad, depressed, and downcast, so he told himself (his soul) to smile and be hopeful in God.

If you know the power of hope and faith you don't have to wait for your circumstances to change to start celebrating. Even as I write this book, we are waiting for a pathology report on a member of our family that could mean serious trouble if it doesn't come back negative. We trust God and keep rejoicing in Him because it makes no sense to do anything else. All of our lives are filled with ups and downs, but we don't have to go up and down with them. We can remain stable in God! God is smiling over us and we can smile back at Him! Since God sits in the heavens and laughs at His enemies surely we can smile (see Ps. 2:4, 37:13).

> If you know the power of hope and faith you don't have to wait for your circumstances to change to start celebrating.

Good News!

Richard J. Foster reminds us in his book that celebration is at the center of God's heart. Jesus entered the world on a note of celebration: "I bring you good news of a great joy," cried the angel (Luke 2:10). Jesus also left the world bequeathing his peace and joy to the disciples. "Peace I leave with you: My [own] peace I now give and bequeath to you" (John 14:27). "These things I have spoken to you, that My joy may be in you, and *that* your joy may be full" (John 15:11).

Jesus began His public ministry by proclaiming the year of Jubilee. He wanted people to realize that a perpetual jubilee (celebration) of spirit was now available. Captives were released, debts were canceled, the blind received their sight, the oppressed were liberated, and the poor received good news (see Luke 4:18–19). Jesus wanted the people to know that they no longer had to worry and be anxious. They could trust Him to take care of them and this formed the basis for celebration. The burden of fixing everything that was not right in life was no longer theirs. They could live without fear! They could cast their care on Him and live in celebration.

"Celebration is central to all the Spiritual Disciplines. Without a joyful spirit of festivity the Disciplines become dull, death breathing tools in the hands of modern Pharisees. Every disciple should be characterized by carefree gaiety and a sense of thanksgiving," says Richard Foster.[1] It is vital that we discipline ourselves to celebrate; otherwise, we won't be able to maintain any of the other disciplines that are necessary to successful living.

The media today fills the world with bad news. They report every tragedy, murder, and theft. They run and rerun reports of politicians and other leaders who are dishonest and immoral. There is nothing uplifting about the evening news on television or in the newspapers, but I have a book on my lap right now

that is filled with good news! It is the Bible and it is the book
I base my life on. Jesus came to bring good news! He preached
good news! The world we live in and our lives are not hopeless
because Jesus is alive! He is the light in darkness and hope to
the hopeless.

There are good things taking place all over the world, but the
media rarely report them. For example, we just got the pathology report back on our family member and it was all negative.
The news was good! We should all tell and retell every good
report we hear. We should war against the prevailing spirit in
the world of sadness, depression, and fear with a genuine spirit
of celebrating what God has done for us and what He is doing
every day of our lives. I have decided to swim upstream against
the negative current in our society. Let's stay on the narrow
path that leads to life together, and avoid the broad path that
leads to destruction.

Let us join with the Apostle Paul in his declaration to celebrate life no matter what was going on around him: "But none
of these things move me; neither do I esteem my life dear to
myself, if only I may finish my course with joy and the ministry which I have obtained from [which was entrusted to me
by] the Lord Jesus, faithfully to attest to the *good news* (Gospel)
of God's grace (His unmerited favor, spiritual blessing, and
mercy)" (Acts 20:24, emphasis mine).

*   *   *

Sometimes by the time we get to the end of a book we have
taken in so much information that we may have forgotten the

main points that the author was hoping to make. I don't want that to happen with this book, so I would like to remind you of a few things:

1. Eat the cookie...buy the shoes! The cookie is only a symbol of a principle that I am sharing. Do something that you like and enjoy, and don't feel guilty about it. Don't let the workaholic and out-of-balance people in your life make you feel guilty, either.

2. If you don't know what you enjoy because you haven't taken time to enjoy much of anything in your life, then start experimenting and find out. You may even have to develop interests, but whatever you need to do, do it and refuse to live without celebration.

3. Reward yourself for progress and stop punishing yourself for everything you view as a mistake or a failure. Remember that you never really fail if you keep pressing forward and God is ready to forgive your faults, mistakes, and sins if you will simply ask Him to.

4. Learn to lighten up! Don't be so intense about life's problems and challenges. It is doubtful that they will ever all go away, so we need to learn to co-exist with them joyfully.

5. Celebrate discipline because it is your friend and not your enemy.

6. Discipline yourself to celebrate, because God loves a party!

7. Celebrate you because you are worth it!

8. Celebrate Jesus because He is the absolute greatest and most awesome gift that we have.

Well, the book is finished and I am going to celebrate! Friends are coming to visit and I told them to bring my cookie! If you are wondering about this cookie, it is something called a "double-doozie," and it is two chocolate chip cookies with icing in the middle (you should try one). I do discipline myself to eat only half of one because the last time I ate the whole thing it nauseated me. To finish writing an entire book deserves more than half of a cookie, so I am going out to dinner with some of my family and I am going to laugh as much as possible. After dinner I am going to watch a good movie. Yesterday I celebrated almost being done with the book by taking my two wonderful daughters-in-law shopping. I am determined to find something to celebrate every day of my life and I invite you to join me in my quest.

NOTES

11. Give Your Soul a Vacation

1. Vine, W. E., *Vine's Expository Dictionary of New Testament Words: A Comprehensive Dictionary of the Original Words with Their Precise Meanings for English Readers* (MacDonald Publishing, 1989).
2. Nee, Watchman, *Balanced Christian Life* (Christian Fellowship Publishers, New York, 1981).

12. Priorities

1. Tozer, A. W., *The Pursuit of God* (Christian Publications, New York, 1948), 101–102.

15. Celebrate Discipline

1. Foster, Richard J., *Celebration of Discipline: The Path to Spiritual Growth* (Harper San Francisco, San Francisco, 1983), 1.
2. Ibid., 9.
3. Maxwell, John C., *Failing Forward: Turning Mistakes into Stepping Stones for Success* (Thomas Nelson, Nashville, 2000).

16. Discipline Yourself to Celebrate

1. Foster, Richard J., *Celebration of Discipline: The Path to Spiritual Growth* (Harper San Francisco, San Francisco, 1983), 191.

ABOUT THE AUTHOR

JOYCE MEYER is one of the world's leading practical Bible teachers. A #1 *New York Times* bestselling author, she has written more than eighty inspirational books, including *The Love Revolution*, *Never Give Up!*, the entire Battlefield of the Mind family of books, and two novels, *The Penny* and *Any Minute*, as well as many others. She has also released thousands of audio teachings, as well as a complete video library. Joyce's *Enjoying Everyday Life*® radio and television programs are broadcast around the world, and she travels extensively conducting conferences. Joyce and her husband, Dave, are the parents of four grown children and make their home in St. Louis, Missouri.

OTHER BOOKS BY JOYCE MEYER

Hearing From God Each Morning Devotional
The Love Revolution
Any Minute
New Day, New You Devotional
I Dare You
The Penny
The Power of Simple Prayer
The Everyday Life Bible
The Confident Woman
Look Great, Feel Great
Battlefield of the Mind*
Battlefield of the Mind Devotional
Battlefield of the Mind for Teens
Battlefield of the Mind for Kids
Approval Addiction
Ending Your Day Right
21 Ways to Finding Peace and Happiness
The Secret Power of Speaking God's Word
Seven Things That Steal Your Joy
Starting Your Day Right
Beauty for Ashes (revised edition)
How to Hear from God*
Knowing God Intimately
The Power of Forgiveness
The Power of Determination
The Power of Being Positive
The Secrets of Spiritual Power
The Battle Belongs to the Lord
The Secrets to Exceptional Living
Eight Ways to Keep the Devil Under Your Feet

Tell Them I Love Them
Peace
*If Not for the Grace of God**

J OYCE M EYER S PANISH T ITLES

Las Siete Cosas Que Te Roban el Gozo
(Seven Things That Steal Your Joy)
Empezando Tu Dia Bien (Starting Your Day Right)

*Study Guide available for this title.

B OOKS BY D AVE M EYER
Life Lines